UNDERSTANDING BODY SIGNS AND LANGUAGE

The Ultimate Guide To Speed Reading Body Language Easily

John
Mario

Table of Contents

Foreword

Our body language, the way we use parts of our body when we are out in public, is a huge sign of how we are feeling. Experts have noticed how you can see what a person is thinking just by looking at their body. It's known as body language reading, but you don't want to be noticed doing it. There are subtle signs that people reveal all the time, and it only takes a second to read them. For example, watch the way someone moves their eyes when listening to you or how they hold their lips when speaking. Their stance and hand movements are also telling. All of these tiny bits can give big answers if you pay attention and know what to look for!

This eBook is about leveraging body language reading for your benefit. You'll learn the signs people give off when reacting to you, so you can dive into someone's mind. Imagine all the things you can do with this power - even talk people into agreeing with your ideas before they even voice any hesitations! Not only will you be able to better understand those around you, but it'll also help boost your confidence and enhance your reputation in society (especially important if you're in the public eye). Now, keep in mind that not everyone behaves normally - there may be exceptions here and there - so use your best judgment.

Finally, being aware of how body language works gives you an opportunity to make sure yours works for you too! You know what signals to give off and therefore can manipulate those signals to make sure people get the message you want them to receive. This book is extremely valuable; it'll help build stronger relationships by understanding what's on people's minds, as well as help improve your image in society – get reading!

Chapter 1:

Basic Principles of Body Language

Before we dive into our amazing techniques, let's talk about reading body language. It's essential to understand this concept before attempting to interpret what people are feeling. This introductory chapter will explain the principles behind it and what you should look for when speed-reading someone. Here's a quick overview of body language and some things to consider when trying to interpret it.

Basic Principles of Body Language

In both formal and casual communication, there is a lot of emphasis on words or what people say. However, nonverbal communication is equally or perhaps even more important. Body language says a lot, and many times, what it says is more important than the words actually spoken.

Suppose someone says "I am happy to welcome you into my home." But if the arms are crossed over the chest, the body is in a rigid body, and the face is indissoluble, the opposite word will meet his words. a man will speak so that he sees and feels this, and so acts;

Recognizing the power of nonverbal or body language, they have long studied the field of psychological science they call kinesics. This refers to body language as a significant communication and extension factor in human relationships. For example, for managers and leaders, understanding body language is important. Nonverbal gestures and affirmations help them value their employees and evaluate the emotions or thoughts of people on the board.

From the interview process to the time an employee resigns or is fired, their body language is seen and "heard." Outside of the work environment, nonverbal language is equally important. Everyone's family, parents, children, lovers, spouses, neighbors, friends, enemies - communicate through non-verbal communication. And although they are silent, nonverbal messages are often loud, clear, and unmistakable.

A teenager who storms off and slams doors, lovers who exchange tender looks and a mother who anxiously waits for her daughter to come home—these don't even have a single word to accurately communicate their feelings.

Therefore, the first principle of body language is this: -

Body signals reveal true feelings and thoughts.

Good numbers of people, under regular conditions, are not deliberately aware of their body language. As such, they do not often use body language to lie or cover up the truth. This means that compared to words, body language tends to be a more accurate reflection of what they truly feel or think. In cases when what a person says is different from what his body language says, trust the nonverbal message more than the actual words.

How to read body language correctly is a skill that is developed through experience, practice, and careful observation. Being observant is especially important to learn how to correctly interpret nonverbal language.

One should know that it is not just the facial expressions, the body stance, or the movements of the limbs that comprise body language. Here are other elements of nonverbal communication:-

• The distance or space between the people communicating (also called proxemics)

• The breathing or respiration of the person, and other signs if present or noticeable: perspiration, blushing, pulse rate

• The quality of his voice (pitch, pace, volume, intonation, pauses and others)

• How a person holds or touches certain things such as a pen, cigarette, bag or his glasses.

Being observant means noticing all these, in addition to the facial expressions, of course, and the movements of the body. Through studying body language, one can further learn intricate varieties and details of these general expressions that convey different meanings.

Chapter 2:

How to Read Body Language

Now that you're familiar with body language, it's time to begin with our strategies. Reading body language has many approaches. - you should be able to spot the clues - but keep in mind that there can be exceptions. Nonetheless, these signs are typically universal and you can use your intuition to figure out what people are trying to express, often without words. Let's start with the various tips and techniques on how you can interpret body language from those you encounter.

How to Read Body Language

For those interested in reading body language, there are certain skills that need to be developed. Being observant and committing to the learning process are essential, as it takes careful study and patience to master this art. Nevertheless, it is not a very difficult task due to the research on this topic performed by psychologists and scientists, which has provided considerable guidance. Additionally, it is an inherently fascinating and useful skill. We all want to know when someone is lying or hiding their thoughts, after all.

Here are some tips to improve your body language skills: Start by noting the eyes, as they are often seen as 'the windows to the soul' and convey a lot of how a person feels inside. Secondly, pay attention where their eyes may be directed - if they seem to look away often, it could mean guilt or hiding something. Facial gestures can also give away clues; for example, rubbing the chin can indicate thinking or quick eyebrow movements indicate surprise. Further still, observing body positioning can tell you how two people feel about each other - the closer the better! Finally, hand movements too can express much about a person's inner emotions - although there's too much detail for this piece! To learn more about body language reading, check out some books on the subject and practice observing people around you - with enough time you should become quite skilled!

Chapter 3:

How to Speed-The Real People's Minds to Enhance Our Lives

Reading body language is one skill, being able to do so discreetly is a whole other level. When you're reading someone's thoughts, you need to be careful not to stare. them down as that will make them very uncomfortable. Your reading needs to be fast, like a glance, that way the person doesn't feel like you're trying too hard. You also need to remember not to linger your gaze on any part of their body as it will give off the wrong impression. This chapter will teach you how it can be done; with this skill, you can quickly interpret someone's message without words and tailor your response accordingly for optimal results.

How to Speed-Read People's Minds to Enhance Our

Lives

On a daily basis, we come across a variety of people in our lives- whether it be for business, education, or simply discussing with family and friends. In these situations, we may have an offer or request that we'd like them to accept or decline; this is where basic mind reading tricks can come in handy. Those who know how to preform this feat can easily understand what the other person is thinking and feeling; such techniques are incredibly helpful in day-to-day life.

Meditative Practices

Yoga and meditation are great ways to learn how to read a person's mind. Taking meditation classes can help discipline your mind and make it more conscious. In an Alpha state, which is between being awake and asleep, people are more receptive to impressions and relaxed. This state can be achieved in daily life, like when one becomes drowsy while watching television or driving. However, regular practice of yoga or meditation can lead to alertness, allowing you to easily sense others' minds and comprehend their reactions.

Putting Ourselves in Their Shoes

To read someone else's mind, try to put yourself in their shoes. Studies and research have shown that when we observe someone doing something we've done before, our brains alert us. With this knowledge, we can interpret the thoughts, emotions and reactions of others.

The Importance of Numbers

Developing the skill of speed-reading people's minds is a very beneficial ability. To do so, you should strive to build a large network of friends, acquaintances, and other contacts with which you communicate regularly. By doing this, you will gain a better understanding and knowledge of people in general and their behaviors and thought processes. With time, this knowledge will help you to decipher the thoughts of others without being fooled or trusting those that are not trustworthy. All this practical experience is essential for developing the skill of understanding people quickly.

Chapter 4:

The Role of Eyes in Body Language

Eyes have always been an expressive part of the human body - poets have written odes to them and medical professionals have done extensive research. Even without a specific knowledge of reading body language, you can recognize many of the signals that people give out just by looking at them. You know that when someone crinkles their eyes, they must be thinking hard, and when they roll their eyes, it usually means they don't agree or approve. These are all quite obvious indications, yet there is so much else that can be conveyed through our eyes. It's only fitting that we start learning about body language with our eyes - if we're willing to listen, there's a lot they can tell us!

The Role of Eyes in Body Language

The eyes are quite expressive, and many believe that the truth can be seen in them. This is why "look into my eyes" has become a familiar phrase that suggests looking for honesty.

Body language experts concur, as eyes can often give away inner thoughts and feelings. People seem to have an innate ability to understand communication through the eyes, even at a distance. We know what a glazed or blank stare means, what it looks like when someone is surprised or feeling strong emotion, and even when they're trying to hide something out of guilt. All these signs are there but hard to explain logically- we just know them by instinct.

Moreover, there are also more subtle movements in the eyes that only those who have studied "eye language" can interpret correctly. For example, if someone's gaze is directed rightward while talking it indicates that the brain is creating something- this could mean fabricating stories or lying. However, if their eyes look left it implies that the brain is recalling information from memory and most likely being truthful about what they're saying. To detect deceit or lack of knowledge detectives and crime investigators take notice of where someone's gaze goes while answering questions.

However, one must remember that right-looking eyes don't always mean lies; it could simply mean that the person does not know the answer or is speculating instead. To properly interpret facial expressions as well as eye expressions takes lots of practice and study.,

Chapter 5:

The Role of Head and Face in Body Language

The parts of a person we can most easily see when we are interacting with them are typically their head and face. Even without trying, we can observe the various cues they give off.

Because of this, it is crucial to comprehend what someone is trying to communicate to us when they are interacting with us.

In this chapter, we'll learn how to interpret what a person's head and face can reveal about their mental state.

Because you don't really need time to comprehend what someone is thinking when they are speaking with you, this chapter on speed reading is crucial.

The Role of Head and Face in Body Language

Universally recognized facial expressions fall into six categories. The following expressions—happiness, sadness or sorrow, disgust, anger, surprise, and fear—are understood by everyone, regardless of race or country of origin. According to scientific theory, everyone is born with the ability to understand these expressions; it cannot be learned.

Beyond these six facial expressions, the head and face are capable of expressing a wide range of ideas and feelings. By carefully studying and patiently observing the people they encounter or come into contact with, anyone can learn about their meanings. This is precisely how body language specialists acquire the ability to "read a person" without the use of words or verbal communication.

The head can give very useful cues about a person's inner feelings and thoughts. First, the general direction of the entire body depends on where the head is pointed. The direction of the head can be forward, left, right, or backward. The meanings of each of these are distinct. Additionally, specific signals produced by head movements like nodding are also helpful in deciphering body language.

Head Signals… What Do They Mean?

Some head movements and their associated meanings are provided below:.

In general, head nodding indicates agreement. Slow head nodding can indicate attentive listening, but it can also be a sign of someone who is feigning interest by doing so out of politeness. The slow head nod is probably genuine if the eyes also show interest. Fast nodding, on the other hand, can convey impatience, as if the speaker is telling the listener to "hurry up!" It also signals to the speaker that he has covered the subject in sufficient detail and should move on to his next point in a conversation.

The opposite of nodding, which expresses disapproval, is head shaking. The head tilting to the side can also convey doubt, annoyance, and frustration.

A raised head denotes alertness, and occasionally neutrality or objectivity. Openly and impartially, the person is hearing you out.

A head held high in the air denotes superiority or arrogance. A protruding chin serves to emphasize this.

Tilting the head to one side can indicate interest and thought. In some situations, it also denotes weakness, complete reliance on the other person, or submission.

Face Signals… What Do They Mean?

Following are some examples of typical facial expressions and their typical meanings.

A smile typically denotes friendliness and cordial behavior. A smile can take many different forms, though. The lack of warmth in the eyes makes it simple to spot a pasted or fake smile. Additionally, this smile is maintained longer than what is normal. A tight-lipped smile denotes feelings that are kept secret and hidden. No teeth are visible, and the mouth is stretched out in a straight line. It appears as though the speaker is conveying the messages, "I don't like you, I don't trust you, and I'm hiding something from you. The twisted smile is an additional type of smile that typically denotes sarcasm.

- The expression of pursed lips frequently indicates that a person is upset, anxious, impatient, or intensely preoccupied with something.
- Lip biting may be a sign of stress. The individual is tense or worried.
- When the lower lip protrudes, someone is upset.

In addition to these, there are a huge number of other facial expressions and gestures that denote particular feelings, attitudes, or thoughts. To become familiar with all of these nonverbal, but incredibly helpful, body signals, it will take a lot of time and study.

Chapter 6:

The Role of Neck, Chest and Back in Body Language

Observing how someone holds their neck, chest, and back while speaking to you can tell you a lot about what is going on in their mind.

If you speak in front of groups, having this knowledge is very beneficial. You can read people's moods by looking at their stances, even from the distance of your dais.

Continue reading to learn more about how someone holds their neck, chest, and back to reveal how they feel about you.

The Role of Neck, Chest and Back in Body Language

Body language is a type of non-verbal communication that most people have at least heard of. Some of it is actually simple to understand. Imagine that you receive a face-slap from someone. Even though they may not have said a word, this suggests that they are upset or angry with you. On the other hand, if someone hugs you and flings their arms around you, it is typically a pretty good indication that they are pleased to see you. Again, they might not have said a word.

However, the majority of nonverbal cues are more nuanced and harder to interpret. Body language and its interpretation have been extensively discussed in literature. Numerous websites and countless books have been written about it. The majority of them will explain how to decipher hand gestures, eye movements, and facial expressions. However, there are other parts of the body, like the neck, back, and chest, that should not be disregarded.

The Neck

Let's begin with the neck. The fact that body language is not a recent phenomenon should be considered. It is as old as mankind. Predators were a constant threat to early man. The trachea is typically torn out by predators when they attack by either going for the side of the neck or the throat. People still hunch their shoulders and droop their chins when they feel threatened. Unaware of what they are doing, they are shielding their throat and covering their jugular vein.

The back of the neck is frequently slapped by someone who is enraged with their raised hand. The urge to hit someone is actually being repressed. Sometimes people will rub their necks to subliminally show that they do not agree with what someone is saying.

A confident or dominant posture is displayed by someone who is slumped over and has both hands clasped behind their neck.

The Back

You can learn a lot about someone by looking at their back. A person who walks or stands with their back straight typically exudes power, pride, confidence, and strength. Their body language conveys the message, "Don't mess with me; I know who I am and what I am. But someone who slouches their shoulders or posture says the exact opposite when they walk or stand. Because they appear to be victims, they are frequently targets for bullies or thugs.

The Chest

A common display of confidence or arrogance among men is to pull their shoulders back and push their chests out. In an effort to impress a person of the opposite sex, both men and women will push their chest out.

Women allegedly exhibit five times as many sexually explicit body language cues as do men. Many women flirt, either consciously or unconsciously, using their body language. A low cut top or dress that exposes a woman's back, chest, or shoulders is frequently worn by women who are flirting. They might raise their hair to show the skin on their neck.

Chapter 7:

The Role of Hands and Arms in Body Language

The hands and arms are among the physical components of the human body—the most obviously physical, that is. That's because most of us have a habit of interacting with others by using our hands and arms in one way or another.

There are numerous ways we use these organs, such as supporting our chin on our hand, keeping our arms at our sides while listening to someone, or keeping our elbows firmly planted on the table. Most of us have a habit of making large hand- and arm- gestures while speaking.

This is a attempt to understand a person's mental state through the way they use their forelimbs. What do all these signals mean? What can these signals tell us about what is going on in their minds?

The Role of Hands and Arms in Body Language

It's a common belief that some people couldn't speak if their hands were tied behind their backs. Even though this statement may be made in jest, it contains a lot of truth. Consider how much your hands are used while you are talking for a moment. The most typical type of body language is probably this one.

It's also interesting to note that gestures and hand signals are the most understandable. For many deaf individuals, sign language serves as their primary means of communication. When there is a language barrier, we frequently use hand signals and gestures to communicate. How many fishermen will show the size of the "got away" fish with their hands?

Nevertheless, there are a lot more, much more nuanced hand and arm gestures in body language. In order to express their positive expectation, people will rub their palms together. In order to appear sincere, place your hands on your chest while speaking. Those who are stressed out frequently hold their hands, while those who are bored may interlace their hands and twitch their thumbs. When someone's hands are clenched into fists while they are seated at a table, it may be a sign that they are tense or anxious, as opposed to when their hands are open, which indicates that they are at ease.

To clearly understand what someone is communicating, you frequently need to take into account multiple body language cues. For instance, if someone stands with their arms crossed in front of them, it usually means they are uneasy, reserved, or have cut you off. However, if the same person were to stand with their legs spread shoulder-width apart and their arms crossed over their chest, they would be displaying toughness or authority. It may be a sign of impatience when someone stands with their hands on their hips. People frequently raise their arms in the air to express their frustration.

Sometimes, to convey a confident or superior attitude, the fingers and thumbs are positioned together to resemble praying hands. It is frequently used by those in positions of authority when directing subordinates. Normally, the person will have their fingers pointing upwards while speaking and downwards while listening.

Another important aspect of using the hands in body language is touch. When you are conversing with someone and they are relaxed, they will frequently lean in your direction and put their hand on your hand or your arm. Particularly between people of the opposite sex, this is true.

People in positions of authority, including police officers, senior military members, head teachers, and even royalty, frequently walk with one palm holding the other hand behind their back. Just observe how frequently someone like Prince Charles engages in such behavior in public.

When speaking, pay attention to the movements of your hands and arms. It's possible that they are merely saying something against your better judge.

Chapter 8:

The Role of Legs in Body Language

Legs have a lot to say about a person's inner nature, just like the arms do. Even when they are just sitting and listening to you, you can tell how they are feeling by the way they use their legs during a conversation.

We will see how there can be various meanings associated with how people use their legs in this chapter. What are these signs that we should be able to understand?

The Role of Legs in Body Language

The legs are the wheels of creativity, according to none other than Albert Einstein. He could have equally well said that nonverbal communication's legs were its wheels. This is because a person's legs frequently communicate what they are not saying.

The majority of the body language knowledge that has been written about is available for free online. Just as many people now intentionally try to control their body language while also trying to observe and interpret the body language of others.

However, the majority of them will focus on their upper body. They will try to control their facial expression and concentrate entirely on what they are doing with their hands, completely ignoring their legs. A clear indication that someone is trying to control their body language is when the legs and upper body are in conflict.

Body language analysis is not a precise science. People respond differently, and so do various cultures. However, you can look for particular signals in the legs and feet. When a man walks with a swagger, it typically indicates confidence. Sometimes women will walk in a way that makes their hips sway. This is a subtly flirtatious indication.

Standing or sitting are the two primary positions for assessing a person's legs. A man should stand with his legs approximately shoulder width apart. It usually means that a person feels grounded and confident if his legs are wider than this. When someone stands with a wider stance, they're trying to make their body appear bigger and more powerful. Along with claiming more space, this stance exudes dominance. Standing with the legs close together or with less space between them than shoulder width could indicate anxiety or inferiority. They are attempting to blend in as little as possible to avoid being seen.

Someone who is sitting cross-legged may be closed off to you or have a closed mind, according to some theories. Getting someone to straighten their legs is a definite sign that they are opening up to you. Just keep in mind that a woman's crossed legs do not necessarily indicate that she is aloof from you.

Women frequently adopt this stance, particularly when sporting a short skirt or dress. She is showing you that she is receptive if her knees are bent in your direction. However, if her knees are turned away from you, it is typically a sign that she doesn't like you and wants to leave.

Look at the feet after moving a little bit further down the legs. When someone points their feet, or even just one foot, in your direction, it indicates that they are at ease around you. When a person's feet point away from you, it indicates that they are getting ready to leave.

Chapter 9:

The Role of the Lips in Body Language

The amount of information a person can convey to you through their lips during conversation is astounding. You will obviously need to read quickly in this situation (which is why we have placed this chapter toward the end of this eBook), as you simply cannot continue staring at their lips. You should be able to tell what the person is thinking with just a quick, casual glance.

But the fact that lips are one of the human body's most expressive parts helps you in this situation. A person cannot maintain a passive mouth when speaking to another person. These are the things you should be looking for because they will undoubtedly move and as a result, will undoubtedly reveal what is happening inside.

The Role of the Lips in Body Language

The three fundamental components of face-to-face communication were identified by UCLA psychology professor Albert Mehrabian. These components, in accordance with Mehrabian, included the words being used, the tone of the voice being used, and nonverbal behavior such as body language.

We send signals through body language, a form of non-verbal communication, frequently without even being aware of it. It frequently manifests in our body language, eye movements, facial expressions, and even gestures. Additionally, it's now considered something of a science to study and decipher body language. Over 80 million websites are devoted to body language, and there are countless books on the topic.

Professor Mehrabian asserts that words make up only 7% of face-to-face communication, while voice tonality accounts for 38%. This indicates that a startling 55% of face-to-face communication takes place nonverbally. Understanding body language is a huge asset. Even though a person may be saying one thing, their body language may be sending a different message.

It is important to recognize right away that interpreting body language is not a precise science. As with different cultures, people react differently. As a result, it might be simple to misinterpret the signals. It is frequently possible to decipher non-verbal communication from facial expressions, particularly those involving the eyes and lips. Even though we may speak with our mouths, the lips frequently convey much more. Lips can be shaped with remarkable precision thanks to the intricate muscles that make them. For instance, pursed lips are frequently a sign of stress. They might be an expression of annoyance or even rage.

The smile is one of the most universally recognized signals across all nations and cultures. It shows amiability and a desire to converse. However, it is not a normal facial expression. We know how to do it. Additionally, a smile might be forced or it might be genuine. Genuine smiles cover the entire face, including the eyes. The only muscles used during an forced smile are those near the lips.

Lip twitching is frequently a sign of someone's inner thoughts. A person may not believe what you are telling them if the corner of their mouth twitches while you are speaking to them. Frequently, when someone is lying, their lips make a brief grimace. Their subconscious is criticizing the lies that they are aware of by doing this.

When interacting nonverbally with people of the opposite sex, the lips in particular are frequently used. A woman who licks her lips while speaking to you frequently conveys interest in you. A slight puckering of the lips into the shape of a kiss is another sign that she is interested in you. But be careful; if her lips are pursed and she touches them with her fingers, she probably feels unsure.

In conclusion, it's important to pay attention to both what people are saying and what their bodies are telling you.

Chapter 10:

Ways to Improve Body Language

You are undoubtedly improving yourself when you are able to read people's body language. Knowing the meanings of various signs will help you avoid giving the incorrect signals.

You're going to use your body as a tool that can communicate to others what you want them to know.

Despite having good intentions, people have frequently given off the wrong signals with their bodies. As a result, there have been broken friendships, failed marriages, arguments among friends, and failed business ventures. That is not something you want to occur to you.

This chapter explains some body language that you can employ to convey the right meaning.

Ways to Improve Body Language

The "Silent Language" is another name for body language. Often, nonverbal communication conveys much more than verbal communication. These days, the majority of people have a good understanding of body language or, at the very least, some knowledge of the subject. It can be helpful or even crucial to be able to read someone else's body language. To be able to read someone like a book is one thing, but how do you know that they are not doing the same thing with you? Does your own body language occasionally fail to support what you are saying or does it occasionally let you down?

You can work on your body language in a number of ways. Keep in mind that most of the non-verbal cues we use to communicate are unintentional. They frequently result from unconscious reactions. Understanding what our bodies are doing is the first step in improving body language.

Learning to control our body language can help us communicate more effectively with superiors or subordinates, during interviews and business negotiations, and when interacting with people of the opposite sex.

Working our way down the body, let's begin at the top. A lot of the time when someone is speaking to you, they want to know that you are paying attention. It will reassure the other person that you are paying attention and that you agree with what they are saying if you simply nod your head slightly. They will feel more at ease as a result, and they frequently say more than they intended to.

Be sure to smile at people with a sincere smile rather than a forced one. Genuine smiles involve not only the mouth but also the eyes. People will feel more at ease with a genuine smile than with a forced one.

Always remember to look someone in the eyes when speaking with them. Do keep in mind to occasionally turn your head, though. You might intimidate someone if you stare at them for an extended period of time.

When speaking to an audience, particularly a group, touch your chest with the palm of your hand. This signal shows that you are being open-minded and truthful. Keep your shoulders back, chest out, and back straight when you're standing or walking. This gives off a strong, determined, and self-assured vibe. Slouching sends the wrong message and makes you seem insecure and weak, which is the opposite of what you want to convey.

You can project the impression that you are in charge of the situation by standing with your feet apart, keeping them at least shoulder width apart, keeping your head high, and folding your arms across your chest. It exudes confidence and assumes a very dominant stance.

Make sure your feet, or at least one foot, is facing the person you are speaking to if you are sitting down. It might seem as though you want to leave if your feet are pointed away from them.

Can one misread another's body language?

Joe Navarro, author of "The Body Language Dictionary," asserted in a Wired magazine interview that "we are never in a state where we are not transmitting information.".

Navarro, a former FBI agent, is well aware of the wealth of information that can be gleaned from gestures, body language, facial expressions, and the tone of voice. He is also aware of how important it is to interpret body language carefully.

Take your spouse's crossed arms as an illustration. It's easy to assume someone is shutting themselves off, but what if they're actually hugging themselves? But could it be that they're sick?

These are frequent false body language narratives, according to Navarro and Eastman. Crossing one's arms and clearing one's throat are two self-soothing or pacifying behaviors that don't always indicate disinterest or deception.

The interpretation we give to others' nonverbal cues can be incredibly deceptive or even ablest.

Let's say that you judge someone to be unfriendly because they do not smile as frequently as you would expect them to. However, it's possible that person may be more kind than you think. In fact, some people have a flat affect, which causes them to express their emotions through their faces less frequently than others.

"The first step in reading behavior is to really understand how frequently you're just so wrong," asserts Eastman.

Now let's review.

Several factors, such as:

- ✓ opersonality.
- ✓ oenvironment.
- ✓ obiology.
- ✓ oculture.

It takes practice, curiosity about human behavior, and the willingness to occasionally be wrong to understand what we say without using words.

It's admirable to want to get better at reading and comprehending body language. You might learn more about the human experience by doing this.

Understanding and Interpreting Body Language.

Although we now know that most of the messages in any face-to-face conversation are revealed through body signals, most people are remarkably unaware of body-language signals and their impact, according to Barbara and Allan Pease in their book.

It takes practice to read and comprehend body language, but it's crucial for a number of aspects of life, such as:

- o showing intimacy.
- o informational provision.
- o professionalism in action.

Here are some suggestions to keep in mind as you work to enhance your nonverbal communication abilities.

Make a recording of yourself.

One of the best methods for improving our body language awareness, according to Blake Eastman, founder of The Nonverbal Group and former adjunct psychology professor at Columbia University in New York, is to record ourselves conversing, either in presentation form or with a reliable friend.

He claims that "raw behavioral data—displayed via video—is the reality of what is happening.".

According to Eastman, watching videos lets us take our time and pay closer attention to the nonverbal cues we use to communicate.

Pay attention to small expressions.

Paying close attention to minute movements, such as head tilts, eye rolls, or slight shifts in the mouth, is necessary to develop your ability to perceive nonverbal communication.

You can get a better sense of what someone may be consciously or unconsciously expressing by paying close attention to their face or body movements.

Look into the theories you have.

Similar to how much of our own body language is automatic, much of how we interpret the body language of others is automatic as well, and this perception frequently goes unquestioned.

You might mistake someone's expression of blankness for disinterest or even rage. However, this isn't always the case. Perhaps they are expressing their contentment in that way, or perhaps their thoughts are elsewhere entirely.

You may think about politely clarifying things when necessary to match emotions to facial expressions in socially acceptable situations. How do you feel about what I just said? is a question that you may want to ask.

Set the context for nonverbal communication.

Depending on the culture and environment, nonverbal communication is interpreted differently.

In some parts of Europe, a kiss on the cheek is a platonic greeting, but in America, it is a romantic gesture. At work, maintaining eye contact may signify polite attention, but in a public park, it may come across as rude.

The unwritten laws of the subcultures and environments you live in must be studied in order to become a student of human behavior through body language.

Affirm that anything can happen.

It's simple to assume that the interpretation we give to an interaction when interpreting nonverbal cues from others is the correct one.

Eastman, who has coached thousands of clients on how to improve their body language, suggests recognizing the things we don't know about other people's communication styles.

"What people want to show and how they show it frequently diverge, according to him."

Beyond behavioral mismatch, it's not helpful to ignore the impact of bad days, illnesses, and distractions that might affect a person's body language in any given interaction.

The ultimate manual on understanding body language and interpreting others.

You need a body language guide because people are difficult to understand.

They almost never express how they truly feel. They make social interactions a guessing game because they keep their true motivations hidden. Can I trust my cofounder? , How does my team actually feel about me and my pitch? , Do these investors like me or my team?

This information is necessary for an entrepreneur. Guessing is too dangerous a game. Relationships that started out with minor misunderstandings eventually broke down completely. You must be aware of what people are really feeling. The secret is being able to interpret their body language.

The nonverbal cues that a person uses can give us insight into their deepest emotions, feelings, attitudes, ideas, and biases. You can tell how someone is really feeling, even when they're trying to hide it, if you know which of these cues to watch out for. Furthermore, the more you understand how another person is feeling, the better you can direct your own behavior.A successful business depends on this feedback loop.

Let's examine a founder's workweek to see the kinds of nonverbal cues that emerge from other people. Yes, people can be perplexing, but fortunately for us, they tend to be predictable perplexes.

This body language guide's content is entirely supported by reputable academic research. Our team of PhDs in psychology and neuroscience has combed through hundreds of papers to identify the best ones. You fully trust the suggestions made.

1. how to tell if someone is paying attention and interested in what you're saying.

Monday: A new Q2 business project plan will be presented. You're presenting a brand-new plan to your team today that is vastly different from what they're used to. You anticipate that only a small percentage of people will be prepared and willing to change. It forces you to carefully consider who is most interested because you only have one or two leads who can be held accountable for the project change.

When a person is interested in something, their body and face will react in a particular way. People are often reluctant to express their interest in an idea or speak up in professional settings. This self-censorship is especially prevalent in relationships between subordinates and executives.

Aside: If this is the case, the first thing to do is to start fostering an atmosphere where speaking up is encouraged (see Sheryl Sandberg and Adam Grant's posts for more information on the benefits of doing this for everyone, as well as the supporting scientific evidence).

But until your company implements this, which requires a lot of conscious effort, it's imperative that you keep an eye out for the subtle nonverbal cues to determine the level of engagement/interest. It can be very expensive to confuse interest with indifference. Keep an eye out for the subtly engaging behaviors.

1. They will slant their bodies forward in your general direction. They, however, are unable to maintain a rigidly held torso position. In contrast, their bodies will be calmer and more composed in contrast.

2. They will exhibit positive emotional indicators such as a real smile (NOT a fake smile; see our other post for tips on how to recognize the difference), a head nod of agreement, and an expression of "positive surprise" with their eyes slightly open.

3. Their body language and facial expressions will both convey that they are paying close attention. This might involve maintaining a straight posture (no hunching over) and making more animated gestures (read our other post to learn more about gesturing and personality types). They may also have a furrowed brow, which is caused by the eyebrow muscle contracting, which is the brain's way of saying, "take in as much of this information as possible.".

This one requires caution because the corrugators muscle is triggered by both anger and alertness. It's not good for anyone to assume someone is interested or attentive when they're actually angry. To get a complete read on the person's state, you must combine the cues. Any of our suggested observations should be followed, and this crucial piece of advice applies. No nonverbal cue is an island, according to a well-known researcher. You run the risk of misjudging the person if you only consider the corrugators. Consider the corrugators as well as the other indicators by using a combined strategy. as follows:

Positive attentiveness equals the corrugators nodding and grinning.

1. Corrugators glaring with unmoving head = hostile.

It's difficult to tell if the dashing Michael Fassbinder is enraged at someone or is truly engaged in what they are saying when looking at the image below, which is a still image where you can't see those other cues. In either case, the same corrugators muscle would be engaged. Therefore, keep in mind to employ the combined approach.

2. How to determine whether someone likes you.

Tuesday: A gathering with a group of investors. Your team has the chance to grow the company, but you still need to secure the next round of funding. You must be aware of who in the meeting finds you (and your idea) appealing. These people will support you and be very motivating. When you speak to them, let their enthusiastic response spur you on to a strong finish.

If you're liked, people will enjoy being around you. We can assume that. Someone who likes you is more likely to enjoy the interaction as a whole. The brain views everything in the environment as more positive (even if those other things aren't that great) when one is in this pleasant "liking" state, known as the "warm glow effect."

When presenting a business idea to a group of investors, for instance, you are much more likely to persuade them if they like you. A bad idea plus your popularity will probably do better than a good idea plus your disapproval. You should always keep in mind how perplexing people are!

Therefore, the first step is to ensure that you have followers (this is outside the scope of this post, but we'll go back to this crucial subject soon, so stay tuned). Finding out if and when someone likes you is step two. Because of our propensity for hiding our true emotions, it is never that simple. This is where paying attention to nonverbal cues can help. Keep an eye out for these things.

a. They will imitate and mirror your body language, gestures, and vocal intonation. The Mirror Neuron System, a network of brain cells thought to be the foundation of all human culture, is involved in this "affiliative mimicry," a natural process that occurs outside of conscious awareness.

This imitating behavior, which is frequently referred to as the "social glue" that holds people together, is linked to a number of advantageous outcomes, such as improved liking, rapport, cooperation, and well-organized work efforts. To test it out, we suggest making a small movement like crossing your legs or lightly bouncing your foot while you're close to someone. Observe the person now to see if they imitate your movement.

Bonus: While speaking, use a word that has multiple pronunciations, such as "process," to demonstrate verbal mimicry. A long or short "o" can be used. See if the other person mimics or copies the way you pronounce it (whether with a long or short "o"). This could be a sign that they like you if they say it the same way they always do.

b. They'll move in closer to you by hunching over. The distance between people is a direct indicator of how much they like each other, according to researchers who have long made this claim. You need to be close to someone without a physical barrier between you and them in order to test this one. Tables and desks are only a hindrance. You are significantly more likely to get a better read on the person and situation if you meet in an area with plenty of open space.

c. They will make fleeting eye contact while speaking and more sustained, direct eye contact while you are speaking.

How to recognize rising tension or hostility.

Wednesday: employee meetings. You've seen some pain points in the way the team interacts with you as your startup business has grown from 2 to 20 in just 6 months. Their actions imply that they might be a little hostile and resentful toward you. You need to be certain in order to put an end to the escalating conflict, but you're not sure—perhaps it's all in your head.

According to scientists, if you closely observe a conflict as it develops, nonverbal cues typically take precedence over verbal ones.

The majority of people aren't very good at recognizing when another person might be moving closer to the area of conflict. It's critical to be aware of nonverbal cues among your expanding team of employees so that you can respond appropriately (ideally in a way that defuses the situation). Numerous well-known angel investors and serial entrepreneurs contend that team conflict is the primary factor in the failure of startups.

It's as straightforward as this: If you ignore warnings of escalating conflict, you run the risk of harming your chances of success. Be alert for these indications.

1. Rather than being fluid and smooth, their body movements will appear less coordinated and almost jerky. Similar to how the body moves, the limbs also move erratically and at odd times. This occurs as a result of the brain's responses becoming less restrained, both in terms of how they are feeling (such as angry or upset) and in terms of the muscles used to move the body.

2. Their eyes will have an indirect gaze, showing more of the sclera (the "whites" of the eyes) than usual.

3. They'll develop a flushed, reddish appearance on their face. The sympathetic nervous system's "fight-or-flight" system, which is preparing the body for an assault or attack, is the cause of this. The face and limbs, which are the areas that require blood the most, are rushed. Although an actual assault is extremely unlikely, the brain still functions in the primitive caveman mode where assaults and attacks were much more common.

How to Spot Dishonesty in Others or Identify a Liar

We are meeting on Thursday to talk about a disastrous product launch. You have a sneaking suspicion that the failed launch attempt was caused by a poor decision made by your marketing lead. You are aware of the person's tendency to downplay prior errors out of fear of failing. Although you want to hear them out and give them the benefit of the doubt, you are aware that they might be lying to cover their tracks.

Research has repeatedly shown that people are generally quite adept at hiding lies in their actual speech. However, the truth can be found in nonverbal cues. The majority of people have limited control over their subtle nonverbal behaviors, so keep that in mind. Consider the following indicators if you want to identify a liar.

i) Their limbs, torso, and body will all seem more stiff, immobile, and tense.

ii) They will exhibit a decreased "blink rate" (we blink at a rate of about 21 bpm normally; a low blink rate is regarded as being between 7 and 10 bpm). According to studies, criminals who lie when being questioned blink less. Politicians are disliked less when they speak without blinking. This occurs because lying takes effort and requires mental energy, which means that less energy is directed toward the muscles that cause the eyes to flinch.

iii) When they have finished telling a lie, their blinking will exhibit a "rebound" effect with rapid blink rates.

Psychopaths are the true exception in this case, which is interesting. They are better at controlling their verbal and nonverbal cues because they are skilled liars. Additionally, they are more adept than average people at detecting deception. They can thus fool and control others for their own gain.

There are many "executive psychopaths" in the business and entrepreneurial worlds, so it's important to take this into account. In fact, according to one study, only about 1 in 100 people in the general population have clinically significant psychopathic traits, compared to about 1 in 5 senior level managers.

But not the murderous psychopaths we see in movies.Violence is only one of eight characteristics that define a psychopathic personality, according to expert Dr. Kevin Dutton (others include cold-heartedness, blame-shifting, and fearlessness; try his Psychopath Challenge). On the subject, books have been written. For more information on this amazing phenomenon, visit these websites. Take a look at this checklist if you think you may know an entrepreneur who exhibits psychopathic traits.

Recap this body language explanation.

Let's review what we discovered about body language reading during the work week. It requires little work but yields big rewards to pay attention to these cues in your everyday interactions. By using these observation-based strategies and tools, you'll be able to gain the valuable insight that so few people possess into the true inner feelings of others.

You will soon be in a position to:

Recognize when someone is paying attention to you or what you're saying (employees may be reluctant to express their disagreement with your idea).

Find out if someone likes you—rarely will someone say out loud, *"I like you,"* or *"I despise you."*.

Understand whether tension or hostility is rising (resolving conflict requires spotting it early, before people even start to express their feelings).

Recognize dishonesty when you see it (people always want to appear honest, but not everyone is).

Recognize if someone isn't trustworthy (people benefit from being seen as trustworthy, but unconscious cues reveal their true intention).

You can now start applying all these techniques to your everyday interactions to gain a better understanding of what the other person is feeling or thinking.

How to spot a dishonest person.

Friday: A gathering of the staff for a weekly huddle. You've noticed that a persistent argument among some of your team members is starting to interfere with business operations. In private, both sides accuse and blame the other of wrongdoing. You need to address this right away because you are aware that someone cannot be trusted.

The most challenging one was left until last. For two reasons, determining trustworthiness is challenging.

First of all, in a lasting relationship, trust is usually built over a considerable amount of time. But in the business world, this luxury is not available. Entrepreneurial decisions, including whether to work with a potential new investor, are frequently made quickly and based solely on intuition. Although gut instincts can be helpful, they are even more potent when supported by science.

Second, there isn't a single cue that indicates whether you should believe something or not. Fortunately, recent research has demonstrated that four cues combined with distrust are reliable indicators. This underlines once more how important it is to read nonverbal behaviors in combination. These four indicators work together to indicate that a person might not be able to be trusted.

a. hand-to-hand contact.
b. Face touching
c. leaning away.
d. Arms crossed.

All four of these had to be present in order for there to be a signal of mistrust, according to a series of experiments conducted by Professor David DeSteno, author of The Truth About Trust. Your brain doesn't make any assumptions when you witness someone touching their hands (without any of the other three). However, your brain sends strong signals informing you that something is amiss when you see someone touch their hands and faces, lean away, and cross their arms.

The researchers used everyone's favorite and beloved robot, Nexi, to confirm their findings using a cunning form of science. They were able to demonstrate with Nexi that the four combinations above were the ones that indicated distrust by turning all the different combinations listed above on and off.

9 Tips To Read People Body Language

A story can be told using anything, including body language, voice pitch, and even facial expressions. We spoke with body language experts about their best advice and techniques for reading people in order to help us interpret those micro expressions.

What is nonverbal communication?

Any type of informational or message-sharing between individuals that doesn't involve using words is referred to as "nonverbal communication. Everything from body language to physical attributes to hand signals can be included. Body language is a type of nonverbal communication that includes physical cues like touch, posture, eye movement, and other physical cues like facial expressions and gestures.

The majority of us have had moments where words have failed us. We become too anxious, timid, or emotionally distraught to think clearly or communicate. Nonverbal cues fill in for us in these circumstances. Conversations are two-sided, so the other person is usually left to interpret those nonverbal cues.

hints for reading people.

1. Recognize positive and negative body language.

Body language expert Blanca Cobb, M.S., says it's common to categorize body language as "negative" or "positive.". informs mbg. It's a typical "negative" expression when someone tenses up; it could be indicative of stress, discomfort, or anger. On the other hand, "positive" body language, such as relaxing the body or taking a comfortable nap, can denote joy and confidence.

We have no control over this advertisement's accessibility features because they are displayed using content from a third party.

2. **Watch the pitch of your voice.**

Depending on how they are feeling, a person's voice can change from its usual pitch. For instance, Cobb notes that when a person is depressed, their voice often becomes lowered. As a result, their voice pitch will be lower and their speech will be slower. Faster, peppier, or cheerier voices typically denote happiness.

3. **Keep an eye on their breathing.**

Cobb claims that when someone is angry, their face may start to turn red. Breathing too quickly usually triggers this response.

The brain releases hormones and neurotransmitters during a fight-or-flight response, and cortisol production increases. Your breathing gets shallow and quick as a result, which also raises your heart rate and blood pressure.

We have no control over this advertisement's accessibility features because they are displayed using content from a third party.

4. **Look at how someone's fingers are curled.**

It may sound strange, but according to Cobb, if a person's fingers have a slight curve, it probably indicates that they are at ease. She explains that it would be strange to walk around with fully extended fingers. "When there is no tension and there is that natural curve, you can tell when someone is feeling okay.

5. Examine their stance.

Someone might lean in if they are interested in you or the conversation. Scott Rouse, behavior analyst and author of Understanding Body Language: How to Decode Nonverbal Communication in Life, Love, and Work, asserts that when flirting, the distance between the flirter and the flirtee will typically get smaller.

In contrast, someone who is fearful or uninterested may lean back. It is critical to pay attention to all context cues, especially in these circumstances.

6. Examine their grip.

In stressful situations, some people extend their fingertips, while others may ball up their fists or tighten their grip. If a person already has a glass or mug in their hand, Cobb warns that they might start to grip it more tightly. Your body needs to let go of this pent-up energy you have. " .

7. Pay close attention to how they move.

A person may show signs of anxiety if they move more than they typically do. The signs of nerves, according to Rouse, can include jiggling the foot or leg, chewing on the lips, wringing the hands, and, in some people, ticks or nervous twitches.

Rouse explains that, in addition to the breathing becoming shallow, the hands and head begin to move erratically. That all depends on how nervous you are, of course. ".

8. The subtleties of their smiles should be noted.

Perhaps, but perhaps not, a person's smile indicates their level of happiness.

According to body language expert David Matsumoto, Ph., there are actually a variety of smiles. D.

Duchene: You can recognize this smile because it typically involves showing teeth and reaches the eyes. It conveys true, genuine enjoyment.

Social: Also known as affinitive or non-enjoyment smiles, these ones are typically toothless, don't extend to the eyes, and are intended to project friendliness and common courtesy rather than genuine happiness.

Dominance: This lopsided smile, which has only one raised corner of the mouth, is more akin to a smirk and is used to express confidence or even condescension.

And just in case you're interested, according to a recent study, the most recognizable flirtatious facial expression is a slight smile accompanied by a sideways head tilt, a slight downward chin angle, and direct eye contact with the object of one's affection.

9. Consider the big picture.

The last piece of advice is unquestionably crucial. Although observing facial expressions can be a useful first step, they aren't always reliable.

"We try to mask it when we feel a certain way but don't want people to know how we feel," Cobb claims. Additional cues, such as pitch and body language. tend to reveal our true emotions. "When interpreting someone's emotional state, it's important to consider the big picture. ".

It's crucial to understand the big picture, whether you're speaking in person or over the phone. In other words, don't just interpret facial expressions. Observe additional context cues, such as verbal or body language cues.

Context's Importance.

Nonverbal cues are easily misinterpreted without context. Crossed arms, for instance, can indicate power and confidence in some situations while signaling resistance and trepidation in others.

When interpreting the nonverbal cues of another person, Rouse advises "remembering to put everything going on around you and that person into context." "The setting has an impact on behavior.".

Making assumptions based on someone's body language can result in misplaced emotions and improper behavior, especially when the assumption is that the person is flirting. Cobb asserts that greeting you and smiling have no sexual connotations. "It's possible that they are friendly. "

Asking questions and getting clarification is crucial before acting in any situation where you are feeling uncertain.

the final conclusion.

People often use nonverbal communication to convey their feelings when they are unable to do so verbally (or when they are trying to deliberately hide them). Understanding these communication cues can improve our ability to understand others.

If you don't understand body language, Rouse claims, "you can't read minds." "However, you can decide more wisely based on what the person you're speaking to or watching is going through or might do next.

Chapter 11

Body Language Analysis in Healthcare:

One form of communication is through body language. Both verbal and non-verbal languages fall under the category of language type. Non-verbal communication, which includes body language, is communication that takes place without the use of words and involves the body's movements and behaviour. Hand gestures, facial expressions, eye movements, tone of voice, body positions, gestures, use of space, and other actions can all be considered forms of body language. Under the umbrella of kinesiology, this study will concentrate on how to interpret body language.

Body language is completely distinct from sign language, which is a full language with its own fundamental rules and intricate grammar systems just like verbal language. On the other hand, body language lacks grammatical rules and is typically a language that belongs to or is categorized according to cultures. Body language can be interpreted differently depending on the culture and the country. Whether body language can be considered a universal language for all people is a subject of some debate. According to some researchers, physical gestures or symbols are used the majority of the time when people are communicating because this interaction of body language allows for quick information transfer and comprehension. Asserts that compared to verbal communication, body language conveys information more effectively. Because of the limitations of physical language, for instance, when someone speaks to someone on the phone about an inquiry, the information is made mysterious. However, there are fewer restrictions and no audience for someone who is seated directly in front of a crowd. Even more so if the speaker is standing, which gives them more mobility, the information conveyed through body language is more readily transmitted and received. As a result, body language improves communication. The purpose of this work is to demonstrate how body language improves workplace positivity.

The effects of human emotions on facial expressions and body movements were the subject of several experiments in. According to the study, body language and facial expressions are reliable indicators of human emotions. It also demonstrated how crucial it is to combine movements of the body with facial expressions and activities to fully understand how people are feeling. To ascertain whether combining the two expressions is required or not, three different stages of experiments were carried out. It was confirmed that connecting them is necessary for identification. It's important to pay attention to eye reading. In expressing and comprehending human emotions, it is regarded as being crucial. Usually, we can infer what someone else wants from their eye movements. Eye language has a variety of outcomes in this regard. The expansion and contraction of the eye size, which are influenced by emotions and enable the observer to convey precise additional information, are suggested by. The average human eye blinks six to ten times per minute. The amount of blinks, however, is less when someone is attracted to someone else.

According to study, body position can be used to recognize and define human emotions. When someone is angry, for instance, they might push their body forward to show dominance over the other person, and their upper body would tilt and no longer be upright. On the other hand, when someone feels threatened by their opponent, they show submission by backing away or cocking their head back. In addition, a person's sitting position can reveal their emotional state. Someone seated on a chair with half of their upper body and head tilted forward demonstrates attention and a desire to understand what is being said. But if they cross their arms and sit with their legs crossed, it suggests that they don't

 Understanding All Body Sign and Language

want to talk and are uneasy with what is being said or the speaker.

Body language analysis is also necessary to avoid misunderstandings regarding the multiple meanings and purposes of a single movement. A person's expressive movement, for instance, might not even be deliberate but rather the result of a physical limitation or a compulsive behavior. Additionally, how someone moves their body may not mean the same thing to another. For instance, itchiness rather than fatigue may cause someone to rub their eyes. Due to the social differences in other cultures, careful analysis is also required. There are movements unique to each culture even though the majority of body movements are universal. This may differ from nation to nation, region to region, and even social group.

A global risk factor that contributes to the deaths of millions of people worldwide is pandemic and epidemic disease. Due primarily to a lack of human and technological resources, the capacity to identify and treat casualties is constrained. Remote diagnosis is necessary when patients are not reachable physically. The face, shoulders, chest, and hands are the four main body regions that exhibit distinct movements in all pandemic and epidemic diseases. Some studies on the reading of these gestures by AI technology have had promising results. In order to identify epidemic diseases early and administer treatment, the concept is to use body language. It should be noted that the COVID-19 disease, which is currently terrorizing the entire world, is the primary and essential catalyst for the proposal of this study. We have a role to play in quickly identifying this disease as information technology and computer science researchers.

Body language analysis's importance.

One of the most important technological advances, artificial intelligence is becoming more and more common and is used in all kinds of applications. AI's use in healthcare is one of its most significant applications. The most crucial aspect of human life on this planet is health. Recently, the use and applications of AI in healthcare have significantly contributed to aiding doctors in the discovery of diseases and the improvement of patient health. The application of AI in healthcare is contingent upon the occurrence of specific symptoms in various body regions. Body language is a manifestation of these symptoms, which have an impact on and reflect in bodily movements and facial expressions. From here, these characteristics of body language can be used to categorize disease symptoms by ML detection. We want to explain the significance of artificial intelligence using body language in this section. AI can analyze certain aspects of body language to address numerous issues in a wide range of applications. For instance, facial expressions can be studied to understand human emotions and use them in psychotherapy or study subjects' emotions. An additional example is the analysis of hand, shoulder, and leg movements and the use of such information to identify useful features in security, medicine, and other fields. From this point on, we want to demonstrate how important body language is and how it can be used for a variety of purposes. We therefore want to propose that ML can also be used to detect body language in order to identify infectious diseases like COVID-19.

The ability to use this technology in healthcare systems is now a reality. Epidemic and pandemic illnesses are regarded as an unsolvable problem that adversely affects human health, which is thought to be the most valuable resource of all. The biggest concern is also the emergence of brand-new pandemics or epidemics that will quickly turn fatal, like COVID-19, which has already claimed close to a million lives. This encourages us to create AI tools that can study patients' body language in order to identify the disease's outward symptoms. This research focuses on general studies that demonstrate the value of interpreting body language across disciplines.

Every computer user uses a mouse and keyboard to interact with the device. Researchers are currently working on a computer system that will allow users to communicate and respond using body language like hand gestures and movement. A thorough review of the published literature was conducted in, which introduced more sophisticated techniques to analyze body language instead of mouse and keyboard movements when interacting with computing devices and recommended the visual interpretation of hand gestures. The issue of robot accuracy recognition was examined in the study by. A fusion system was suggested, with a 99.37% accuracy rate, to identify the different types of fall movements and abnormal directions. Identifying facial expressions and measuring and analyzing facial muscle movements required the development of a facial coding system in. With the help of 1100 images, a database was made. In order to match their movements, the system examined and categorizes creases and wrinkles on the face. The outcomes demonstrated that the performance increased, reaching 92%. Analyzing individual expressions requires integrating facial characteristics and movements with body movements. To test whether facial expressions and body language should be combined, three different experiments were run. The results of all three experiments were positive. A different study concentrated on using deep learning methods to recognize emotions expressed in facial expressions. This study used only convolution neural network techniques to demonstrate how deep learning with these networks successfully recognizes emotions by growing cognition, greatly enhancing usability. In, a brand-new model was created that could recognize physical motions and gestures using two digital video images, providing three-dimensional vector displays.

In order to create a coding system by identifying the minor units of facial muscle movements and then drawing coordinates that defined the facial expressions, the first study demonstrated the relationship between the contraction of the internal face muscles and the facial movements as established by Hjortsjo 1970. Much attention has been paid to the understanding of people's emotions. However, it is still difficult to identify facial emotions and speech expressions, especially among researchers. The research discussed in provided a thorough survey to aid future study in this area. It concentrated on identifying gender-specific traits, creating a framework that automatically determines how emotions manifest physically, and identifying consistent and dynamic body shape remarks. By identifying gestures in pictures or videos, it also looked at recent research on emotion and learning. It was also discussed how to identify the most effective emotions using a variety of techniques that combined speech, body, and facial gestures. According to the study's findings, overtones can still only provide a partial understanding of a person's emotions.

Healthcare Body Language Analysis.

In order to categorize the facial expressions in more than 1100 photographs of people at work, a coding system was developed. A method for analyzing image elements in the gray field, measuring wrinkles, and using a template to create facial movements were three methods that were compared to classify facial expressions. For the three roads, the performance accuracy of the coding system was 89 percent, 57 percent, and 85 percent, respectively; however, when the methods were assembled, the performance accuracy increased to 92 percent. The challenge of online learning is knowing how much student involvement there is in the learning processes. An algorithm is introduced in work to understand student interactions and identify their issues. Two techniques were used in this algorithm to gather proof of student participation: the first used a camera to record facial expressions, and the second used mouse movements to record hand movements. The data were trained by creating two groups, one of which collected facial data while using a mouse and the other without. It was found that the first group performed 94 points (60%) better than the second group, which performed 91 points (51%) better. Work discussed how recognizing facial and speech gestures may offer a thorough analysis of body language. It offered a framework for the automatic recognition of both dynamic and fixed emotional body gestures that combined facial and speech gestures to enhance the ability to recognize an individual's emotions. According to Paper, facial expressions are defined by how they correspond to body positions. The research showed that when the main irritants on the face are similar to those that are highlighted in the body, the effects and expressions are more obvious. However, the model generates various outcomes depending on the properties, whether they are physical, dimensional, or latent. Another important finding from the study is that fear expressions blossom better when paired with facial expressions than when performing tasks.

According to the authors of, the medical advisor must possess engaging communication skills that encourage the patient to make the right choice. They advised doctors to be skilled in using body language such as hand gestures, facial expressions, and eye contact. It was stated that a doctor's smile is the most powerful expression they can use to communicate with their patients because it puts them at ease. The patient answers the doctor's questions with clarity, credibility, and confidence because they feel comfortable, which gives them the appearance of being confident. Furthermore, eye contact between the doctor and patient is crucial for the patient's benefit because a lack of eye contact could imply that the doctor does not value the patient's wellbeing. According to the study, the patient benefits when the doctor uses appropriate nonverbal cues. When a doctor smiles and looks directly into the patient's eyes, as opposed to not looking directly into the patient's eyes, objective data has shown that the patient improves and recovers more quickly and effectively. Additionally, it was found that since the patient is affected by the doctor's voice tone, facial and body movements, and eye contact, patients who receive more attention, feeling, sensation, and participation from the doctor respond better to treatment. Clint reported to work in the intensive care unit for the first time. On that particular day, despite the unit's thoroughness and informational nature, he experienced fear and anxiety. Clint was sitting next to a patient and her sister, contemplating whether it was worthwhile to work in that particular unit. The patient caught a glimpse of Clint's anxiety and nervousness but dared not ask him, so she whispered to her sister that the nurse was anxious. Then, when her sister questioned Clint, "You are worried and anxious today; why; what is there to be so nervous about?" Clint thought to conceal his anxiety and restore confidence; he smiled and responded, "I am not nervous. Nevertheless, there are times when we must pose absurd questions to our patients, which make us uncomfortable. Clint claims that he could tell the patient was stressed out by the way she looked and that he was unable to make her hide it. Clint emphasized that patients' body language and facial expressions have an impact. Through their body language, they can infer their situations. Clint realized his error at this point. His condition might get worse because his patient started feeling stressed and anxious.

Henry stated that treating a patient with behaviors and body language has a greater impact than using drugs in one of his articles [20]. According to the research [21], nonverbal communication between a doctor and patient is crucial to the patient's care. In order to decide on a diagnosis and course of treatment, the doctor can use the patient's nonverbal cues to gather details about the disease's state. According to the research, a patient's ability to communicate nonverbally with a doctor can influence how well they learn about their condition and recover from it. for instance, maintaining eye contact, being close to the patient, and making relaxed-looking hand and facial gestures. According to the research, using nonverbal cues has a beneficial effect on the patient. To expedite patient care, it is advised that doctors receive training in how to effectively use non-verbal cues.

AI-based analysis of the body language of patients.

Body language analysis of patients has been done using a variety of AI methods and techniques. We briefly go over a few studies that have been done in this area so far. A pimple system, which is more specifically focused on facial recognition, was introduced in to analyze facial muscles and, as a result, identify various emotions. The suggested system uses video to automatically track faces and extract geometric forms that represent facial features. The study examined the dynamic information of the facial muscle movements in eight schizophrenia patients. This study demonstrated the capability of identifying engineering measurements for specific faces and pinpointing their precise differences for recognition purposes. measured facial expressions to define emotions and identify people with mental illness using three different techniques. The proposed facial action coding system from the study made it possible to interpret emotional facial expressions, which advanced our understanding of therapeutic interventions for people with mental illnesses.

Many people experience nervous system imbalances, which can cause the patient to become paralyzed and fall without warning. The goal of the study (24), which used a platform (R), was to increase the rate of early warning sign detection and identification. On the waist and chest, wireless sensor devices were positioned. The gathered data were transformed into an analysis algorithm that extracted them and activated them if there was a risk. The findings demonstrated that the patient who was at risk made certain customary movements that suggested a potential fall. The authors also recommended using this algorithm to predict seizures in patients who already have them in order to notify the emergency services of an impending attack.

According to research, a computational framework was created to track the movements of senior citizens and detect organ failures and other sudden declines in vital bodily functions. By using sensors positioned on various body parts, the system tracked the patient's activity and determined its intensity. The experiments demonstrate that this system has a 95.8% accuracy rate in real-time location identification. Another strategy based on data analysis was put forth in for an intelligent home that uses sensors to track the movements and actions of its occupants. This system assists in identifying behaviors and predicting diseases or injuries that residents, particularly elderly people, may develop. In order to monitor their patients' progress and provide remote care, doctors can benefit from this study. The target object capture setup model put forth in is based on the candidate region-suggestion network to identify the manipulator's grab position in conjunction with data for color and deep image capture using deep learning. By combining data for a color image, it was able to detect crawl targets with a success rate of 94.3% on multiple target detection datasets. The research project's goal was to compare automated learning algorithms used to monitor the elderly body functions and movements. The paper under review addresses the elderly and their struggle to maintain independent living without needing the help of others. The support conveyor algorithm, which used reference traits, produced a 95% accuracy rate, which was the highest of the eight higher education algorithms examined.

Certain jobs necessitate extended periods of sitting, which can cause spinal damage and neurological disorders over time. With the aid of sensors attached to the chair, sitting position monitoring systems (SPMS) can measure a person's position while they are seated. The proposed method's disadvantage was that it needed too many sensors. Created an SPMS system that only needed four of these sensors to solve this issue. Through the application of several machine-learning algorithms to measurements of the average body weight, this improved system defined six different sitting positions. The positions were then examined and categorized into any approach that would result in the highest level of accuracy, ranging from 97.20 to 97.94 percent. Medical staff members, hospital equipment, and potential bodily harm are among the worries that hospital doctors in most hospitals have when treating patients with mental illness. The study developed a method to examine the patient's movements and determine the likelihood of harmful behavior by extracting visual data tracking the patient's movements from cameras installed in their rooms. The suggested technique collected the movement points, extracted their properties, and traced the movement points. The movement points' characteristics were examined in terms of their spacing, location, and speed. According to the study's findings, the suggested method could be used to investigate features and traits for various other purposes, such as evaluating the severity of the disease and figuring out its rate of progression. According to the study, wireless intelligent sensor applications and devices were created to monitor patients' health more effectively, aid in disease diagnosis, and provide better patient care. On the patient's body, wireless sensors were implanted to continuously monitor their health, update the data, and send it to the service center. To monitor patient behaviors and compare them to the historical data that has been stored, the researchers looked into the multi-level decision system (MDS). The decision-makers in the medical centers were able to recommend treatments thanks to this information. The

 Understanding All Body Sign and Language

suggested system could also save new disease data, track new cases, and lessen the effort and time required for doctors to examine patients. In terms of patient monitoring and prediction, the results were accurate and trustworthy (MDS).

The application of the short-time Fourier transform was suggested in the study of to track the patient's voice and movement using sensors and microphones. The system successfully identified the patient's conditions by analyzing sound and accelerometer data transmitted by the patient. Regarding the identification of full-body expressions, three experiments were carried out. In the first experiment, body language was matched to incorporate all emotions, with fear being the hardest to convey. The second experiment, which was ambiguous because it focused on facial expressions that were strongly influenced by physical expression, was conducted at the same time. In the previous experiment, focus was placed on vocal expressions of tone in order to pinpoint bodily-related emotional states. Finally, it was determined that in order to reveal true body expression, it was crucial to combine the findings from the three experiments.

At the MIT Institute, an important study was carried out to create a system that analyzes data on brain activities using a wearable device to scan brain nerves to detect pain in patients. The ability to diagnose and treat patients who have lost consciousness and their sense of touch has been demonstrated. In this study, several fNIRS sensors were placed on the patient's forehead to measure the activity of the frontal lobe, and ML models were created to ascertain the levels of oxygenated hemoglobin associated with pain. The findings demonstrated that 87 percent accuracy was achieved in detecting pain.

The heartbeat was regarded by the study as a form of body language. Heartbeat monitoring is an essential component of a medical examination. In order to classify the vibration signals of regular and irregular heartbeats through an electrocardiogram, the researcher proposed a one-dimensional (1D) convolution neural network model, CNN. The de-noising auto-encoder (DAE) algorithm was used to classify the heart's sound signals, and the results showed that the proposed model could do so with up to 99 percent accuracy.

Chapter 12

Reading body language with emotional intelligence

According to studies, up to 50% of what you want to say is conveyed through your body language. You can begin to discern what someone might be truly feeling by observing their body language. A few crucial body language cues to look out for are listed below.

Hands on hips or folded arms, a racing heart, perspiration, rapid breathing, clenched fists, and fixed eyes are all signs of anger.

Open arms and legs, a smile, a relaxed body posture, and long-lasting eye contact all signify happiness.

- **Anxious:** racing heart, rapid breathing, and agitation.

- **Fury** is characterized by a stern, fixed gaze and loud, rapid speech.
- **Sadness** is exhibited by a sagging body, glum eyes, and a closed mouth.
- **Eyebrows** raised, wide eyes, an open mouth, and a backwards jerk are signs of surprise.

Indicators of embarrassment include a red or flushed face, an averted gaze, avoiding direct eye contact, and a fake smile or grimace.

When working face-to-face, the majority of employees have a natural understanding of these non-verbal cues—all the ways in which we communicate without words. Examples include a coworker's nod or grimace, a colleague's uncomfortable shift in a chair.

The majority of us have learned social skills, which means we can interpret others' non-verbal cues with some proficiency and can also communicate ourselves non-verbally. Consider your innate ability to, for example, smile when you greet a client, make eye contact when you speak, and maintain a confident demeanor when you are being interviewed.

According to Mi Ridell, a body language specialist based in Stockholm, Sweden, "if you want to influence people in a positive way, then your attitude and how you are perceived using non-verbal communication is very important.". People frequently respond to your actions more than your words, according to Dutch nonverbal communication expert Annemieke Meurs-Karels, "because it communicates the underlying message - what you really think and feel, and your intentions.".

Although we've been taught the value of non-verbal cues in face-to-face interactions, this type of communication can seem less significant in a virtual setting. Online chats are now commonly used for business conversations, and meetings can even be held without cameras. However, non-verbal communication still takes place, even when working remotely seems to exclude subtle cues. 92 percent of managers believed that employees who turned off their cameras during meetings were less likely to have a long-term future at their company, according to a 2022 survey of 200 executives.

Workers can gain an advantage if they understand how these subtle signals are changing. The change in non-verbal communication is yet another disruption to keep up with in the new workplace.

Presently Occurring nonverbal communication.

There are two aspects to nonverbal communication.

You have to consider how other people see you as well as how you interpret other people based on their own nonverbal cues. According to Meurs-Karels, it is not an exact science because there is a lot of ambiguity in how you might interpret someone's signal compared to how another person might; it frequently depends on your personal experiences and relationship to the communicator. Of course, if you're the one speaking, the same could happen to you.

Despite these subjective differences, the experts claim that non-verbal cues have significant meaning for both parties and that it is crucial to pay attention to them in any work setting, whether in-person or remote.

Of course, there have always been aspects of nonverbal communication that don't take place in face-to-face interactions. These subliminal cues could, for instance, start with a profile picture on a resume or job-search website. Even choosing whether or not to use an emoji in a work group chat can alter the atmosphere of the conversation. However, we often think of nonverbal communication in terms of our face-to-face interactions. For instance, we may try to decipher attitudes from the firmness of a handshake or look for significance in how closely coworkers sit when working together.

However, the new workplace changes in terms of where and how we work have greatly expanded the field of nonverbal communication.

For instance, in video calls, backgrounds can convey a variety of nonverbal cues about coworkers' lifestyles, interests, and even levels of professionalism. Non-verbal cues now have a different home, and we place different weights on them as a result of our increased reliance on text communication, such as messaging apps. Body language, such as eye contact, posture, gestures, and facial expressions, as well as personal grooming, like the hairstyles or clothes we choose to wear to work, have all made an appearance in digital communication.

But even as we retrain our brains and improve our ability to decipher others' non-verbal cues in the digital world, perfecting our own online communication may require some practice. "In the digital setting, we have to think about the setup and accept that it's a new way to communicate," says Ridell. She says, "We have to learn some new techniques, they don't come naturally.".

What makes it crucial now?

Although we are largely trained to decipher traditional non-verbal cues, this new form of communication in the digital age is still not completely second nature to many.

For instance, it is common for such rules to be broken while on a video call. However, if a colleague places their camera below the chin, forcing people to look up at them, "we don't like them as much as if they are on the same level," says Ridell—the same thing that occurs in person. In fact, research demonstrates that during video calls, elements like camera angles, proximity to the camera, and the ability to make eye contact all affect how likeable people are perceived.

Particularly, eye contact is associated favorably with likeability, social presence, and interpersonal attraction. On a video call, however, we must overcome our innate tendencies if we want to make eye contact. When it's your turn to speak, you must learn to look into the camera because, according to Ridell, "the brain wants to look at the face [on the screen]. "

Therefore, ignoring the value of tacit communication in a remote setting can have unintended consequences, such as disengaged employees or workers who lack the appearance of professionalism when using a particular video-call background.

However, there is a benefit to taking into account non-verbal behavior, just as you would in person: simple non-verbal cues like leaning in rather than slouching back or visibly grinning during a joke during an online meeting can help show engagement and promote connections. It can also be a matter of politeness when making gestures like turning on the camera. In a board meeting, "we wouldn't sit with a bag over our heads," asserts Ridell. "In order to stop acting rudely, we must learn new rules. ".

Similar to how using a clear photo of your face with an open expression rather than an empty avatar photo on a chat channel may seem like a small gesture, it can help forge bonds even with coworkers you haven't met in person. According to Ridell, viewing a photo can increase your sense of trust in a person. That's not to say that you should always be face-to-face with coworkers; a well-placed emoji or gif in a group chat can also have a significant impact on others and foster a welcoming, inclusive environment.

Maintaining solid relationships in the digital sphere is challenging, but trying to communicate nonverbally can be helpful. "A lot of useful contact with employees, colleagues, and clients happens through non-verbal communication because it's a way to read each other's emotions," claims Meurs-Karels. "Observing what's happening with one another is even more crucial in the digital age, where people spend their days alone in their homes. ".

"The need to understand one another won't go away."

In the end, nonverbal communication may feel like more work in the digital world, but employees can benefit from how others perceive them and promote genuine connections.

Making a conscious effort could entail taking a few minutes to create a profile picture that looks professional, checking that your camera is at the proper height before a meeting, or adding a few encouraging emojis to a group chat. According to Ridell, seemingly insignificant actions can have a big impact by encouraging employees to "be more alive in a digital context and to show some passion and compassion.".

Being willing to engage nonverbally makes it simpler to understand others and to be understood in the modern world, where workers sometimes find it difficult to decode one another and where isolation can flourish.

Being open to sharing a bit of yourself with others and giving others your full attention is a necessary part of effective nonverbal communication. Individuals and teams can benefit long-term from developing these skills in the digital world. According to Meurs-Karels, "society is moving more toward online communication and away from face-to-face communication.". The need for communication, however, will always exist. ".

How to interpret the body language of your relatives.

Families come to you as a funeral director with a long list of requirements and a tight timeline.

A highly personalized ceremony for someone you've never met must be planned in a matter of days using only their will (if they have one) and a group of people you may have only recently met.

Being able to read a family's body language can be crucial because people who are grieving a loss frequently find it difficult to provide you with the information you require. We've put together a few body language reading pointers that ought to help you comprehend your families better.

Comfort/Discomfort.

One of the best ways to read someone's body language is to assess whether they seem comfortable or uncomfortable as a whole, rather than focusing on particular gestures or stances.

If, during a meeting with a family, one member is speaking exclusively while another sits there with their arms crossed, a worried expression, or refuses to look at anyone, that should raise suspicions. Perhaps they are concerned that things aren't going as they should but are too afraid to express it.

On the other hand, if someone nods their head and seems to be enjoying the conversation, you can be sure that everyone is on the same page.

Examine Sadness.

When it comes to reading body language as a funeral director, the fact that the families we serve are frequently depressed during our conversations has a significant impact. It can be difficult to tell whether someone is simply sad about their loss or whether they are uncomfortable with the conversation.

Check the person's body language to see if it's tight or loose for a hint. They are probably uncomfortable if they are tense, such as with their fists crossed or their jaw clenched. If their posture is relaxed—shoulders hunched, brow furrowed, hands outstretched—they are probably just depressed.

Think about interaction.

When two people are conversing, it can be simple to tell how involved they are by their interactions with one another.

When someone is on board and supportive of you, they:.

* Make a head nod.
* Take a good look at you.
* slant your body in your direction.
* Be friendly and laid-back.
* If someone is not listening to you and agreeing with you, they:
* Don't nod their heads and might even shake them.
* Look away frequently—off to the side or downward.
* Steer clear of you.
* are uncomfortable and restricted.

Even if someone claims to agree with you or to like your idea, their body language may betray this. To make sure that everyone is on the same page and receiving what they want or need, it's critical to pay attention to these cues.

Typical Body Language.

Several common body language nuances could aid in your understanding of your families:

Toes pointed away. Out of respect for you, they are talking to you, but they want to end the exchange.

fake grins. It isn't genuine if they smile with their mouth but you can't see it in their eyes. The families you speak to are likely unhappy because of their loss, so you shouldn't worry too much about them being unhappy during the conversation.

o   lips that are pursed. This might indicate discomfort.
o   away, turning. A sign of discomfort could be this.
o   a cross of arms. This may imply dissatisfaction or even discomfort.
o   eye movement. Unease may be indicated by looking away or around.
o   blinking rate increases. This may signal discomfort.

Fidgeting. Fidgeting typically indicates discomfort and includes twiddling hands, tapping feet, shaking legs, and other behaviors.

Every person is unique.

It's important to keep in mind that, even though this advice may be applicable in a variety of circumstances, every person has a unique way of expressing their emotions through body language. Utilize these as a starting point, but also take into account your own gut feeling, and don't be afraid to ask your family members questions to ensure that everyone is on the same page.

Chapter 13

How to teach your child to read nonverbal cues.

People communicate their feelings in addition to using words. Though sometimes kids are unaware of that. You can provide assistance if your child struggles to understand social cues or body language in general.

Coordinate the movement with the message.

Demonstrate to your child how different body gestures can convey a distinct and precise emotion. Put your hands on your hips, tap your fingers, shrug your shoulders, and fidget. Give an explanation of the hidden meaning behind each action. "When a person is standing like this, it might indicate that they are getting impatient. Or your words have upset them. " .

Give instances.

By observing how people interact in real life and on television, you can bring the idea of body language to life. (You can even turn off the sound if you and your companion are watching TV.) Assist your child in identifying hints that point out how each person is feeling. Ask what hints suggested that the person felt that way. Giving your child a verbal anchor will help them remember the visual cue, such as "The man's face was red" or "The girl's fists were clenched.". Practice body language charades.

Kids can better understand the relationship between the two by acting out their emotions through body language. Make it into a game, and invite the entire family to participate. Put each different emotion on a separate index card. These include emotions like joy, sorrow, rage, fatigue, and so forth.

Draw a card and act out the emotion as you go, and the rest of the group tries to guess what it is as you go.

Avoid being too literal.

Teachers who have "had enough" may cross their arms. Or perhaps they're just not very warm. A classmate who is disinterested in the conversation might be clasping his hands behind his neck. Alternatively, he might just be extending.

Your child should be told that gestures and body language alone cannot fully convey an idea. For your child to fully understand what is being said, tone of voice and words must both be taken into account.

There are many things you can do to support your child's social skills. You can see a video about how TV watching can teach your child social skills. Additionally, look up advice on teaching your kid to read facial expressions, comprehend personal space, and recognize subtle voice-tone changes.

Developing Connections with Children: The Value of Body Language.

"Adopt the attitude that you and your child are in charge of handling any problems that may arise as you and your child face the outside world. In The Connected Child, Karyn Purvis advises, "Convey your deep alliance not just in words, but also through body language, posture, and voice."

Both favorable and unfavorable body language.

It matters how you respond to your kids, both verbally and nonverbally. If your child asks you a question and you answer it while still looking at your phone, you might still be giving off the impression that you are bored or irritated. According to experts, this kind of reaction causes your child to experience negative emotions and increases the likelihood that he or she will adopt negative behavior. According to Julie-Ann Amos' article, "Parental Body Language and Children," your child may feel "unwanted, unimportant, or that you simply don't care" if you exhibit negative body language repeatedly over an extended period of time.

The opposite outcome is produced by assertive body language. "Your child will feel more confident and self-esteem if you consistently display open, friendly, and respectful body language toward him or her," says Amos. "He or she is also much less likely to engage in negative behaviors to get your attention.".

Posture.

Your attitude and level of receptivity to those around you can also be inferred from how you sit, stand, or face them. A closed-off demeanor when speaking to your kids will have the same detrimental effects as avoiding eye contact. When you cross your arms or hunch your shoulders, for example, you are closing off the center of your body and displaying disinterest, hostility, or anxiety. A person who is speaking to you should have an open posture, with their body facing them and their exposed midsection. Open positions convey friendliness, openness, and willingness. To strengthen the bond between you and your child, Purvis advises speaking to them at eye level.

According to Deebra Jennings, the Safe Families Program Manager for Covenant Kids, "you have to bring yourself to their level so they feel less intimidated by you.". It's important to communicate with them rather than at them. ".

Voice **tone.**

Numerous studies have shown that kids who have experienced a lot of stress or trauma have a harder time listening. According to a recent study, people find it more difficult to remember information when it is delivered in a fearful or anxious manner.

Researchers from the National University of Singapore argued in a study published in 2012 that while vocal expressions of emotion can draw attention, they can also make it more difficult for listeners to recall the information later on. More negative emotions were linked to information that was retained. Your child will be better able to remember the instructions you are giving them and will behave better if you use a calmer, more neutral tone of voice when speaking to them.

It's true what they say: practice makes perfect.

Using both verbal and nonverbal communication can help you and your child have a better relationship and have fewer behavioral problems. Nonverbal communication cannot take the place of verbal communication. Purvis advises practicing giving instructions while gazing in a mirror in order to hone non-verbal communication skills. She advises her readers to ponder the following.

What message is my child receiving at a primal level? Is the child against me, or are we working together? Am I waving my finger at her? Am I clenching my teeth and adopting an aggressive stance with my hands on my hips?

Being an adult who understands the value of allies, you want to be one of your child's strongest allies.

The Science of Body Language When Giving Patients Diagnoses.

Here, we talk about how important body language is when giving diagnoses to patients.

Even though it may be unfortunate, there are times when doctors must inform patients of bad news. However, how news is conveyed frequently has a significant impact on how it is received. A skilled man relies on the language of the first when his eyes and tongue are speaking two different languages, as Ralph Waldo Emerson once said. ".

55 percent of communication is nonverbal, according to UCLA psychology professor and author Albert Mehrabian. In other words, more than half of the message you are actually conveying depends on elements like posture, eye contact, facial expressions, and hand gestures, regardless of the message you intend to convey.

The ability to communicate nonverbally and verbally is crucial when giving diagnoses to patients. When expressing concrete information—the nature of a patient's condition, the actions to be taken to treat the condition, etc. —verbal messages were discovered to be more efficient. Physicians should be particularly aware of any nonverbal cues they may be unintentionally giving while conveying this message, though.

This does not necessarily imply that doctors should "put on a happy face" at all times; they also shouldn't act as if negative circumstances don't exist. The degree to which body language matches what the doctor is saying, whether it is upbeat and positive or anxious, may have the greatest influence.

There is nothing to worry about; you're going to be completely fine! is what a doctor may tell one of his patients, which is, one would assume, good news. However, if the doctor speaks slowly or is unable to keep an eye contact for a long period of time, the patient might interpret this as worry. The patient may become concerned about what the doctor may not be telling them as a result of the difference between the doctor's verbal and nonverbal communication.

facial expressions are not the only thing.

Contrary to popular belief, which holds that observing someone's facial expressions is the best way to determine their mood, a Princeton University study found that other factors may also be important. In the study, images of people experiencing emotional "peaks" or extremes were shown to the participants. The photos either showed the subject's body only, just their facial expression, or both.

The participants were then asked to choose the emotion they believed the photo's subject was experiencing. Only looking at the facial expression gave a 50/50 chance of getting the answer right. In other words, the participants' chances of being accurate were the same as if they had made their guesses at random. However, the success rates were significantly higher for those who saw the body or the body and the face.

Some suggestions for dealing with patients.

To ensure that the patient is at ease and hears the news in a way that doesn't make an already potentially distressing situation worse, doctors should keep a few things in mind as they interact with patients.

1) Fix your gaze on the other person.

The delivery of a diagnosis by a doctor is arguably the only time when patient and doctor trust is more crucial. The urge to turn their heads away when delivering bad news is strong in many people. Despite this, doctors must make an effort to maintain some eye contact or else they run the risk of coming across poorly. When a patient is already feeling uncomfortable, gaze avoidance, which is frequently a sign of deception, can unintentionally make things worse.

When speaking with patients, PatientPop advises applying the 50/70 rule to determine how much eye contact is "too much.". Make eye contact roughly half the time when you're speaking. To demonstrate that you are paying attention and actually hearing the patient's concerns, increase your listening time to about 70% of the total time.

2) *Be aware of your posture.*

If you're not careful, the way you stand could aggravate an already anxious patient who is receiving a diagnosis for a potential medical condition. A closed position can make the patient feel alone, and standing over them while they are sitting can make them feel as though you are speaking down to them.

Bring yourself to the patient's eye level to foster a relationship of trust that can aid in the patient's recovery. Sit across from them in a chair if they are seated and maintain eye contact often. As you speak, turn your body to face them with an open posture. This helps to demonstrate that you are approachable, that you are a member of the patient's team, and that you are making every effort to assist.

3) *Smile!*

When you tell patients their diagnoses, frowning or scowling either makes you seem detached and uninterested in their care, or it makes the situation seem even more gloomy than it may be. Make sure the smile fits the circumstance and refrain from going overboard. Giving bad news while grinning widely can be just as intimidating as scowling.

The co-author of Words Can Change Your Brain, Mark Waldman, suggests adopting a "Mona Lisa smile" and a soft gaze. "Picture someone you deeply care about or envision an experience that was remarkably satisfying before you enter the room to deliver the diagnosis. This quick exercise can quickly put your mind in a state where the expression in question will come naturally.

FOR EFFECTIVE COMMUNICATION, YOU SHOULD BE AWARE OF 20 BODY LANGUAGE CUES.

For the majority, words are used to start and finish an informational exchange. In reality, there are a lot more things to take into account.

Examining a person's body language can help you determine their true intentions when interpreting what they say or do. Depending on the circumstances, the human body performs numerous unconscious movements.

Indicators of body language can occasionally be blatant and obvious. It's likely that if you see someone crying, they are upset or sad about something. Sometimes it's difficult to read body language signals. For instance, if someone isn't looking at you directly, you might completely miss their mocking eye roll.

There are many different ways to read body language, and each one has value. Understanding body language can help you gain more self-assurance and even increase your chances of winning in negotiations at work and in your personal life.

Whether in business, romantic relationships, or even when meeting someone new, body language cues can be crucial.

Not many people are active listeners, which is surprising. According to the video below, a typical person can speak up to 225 words per minute, but our minds can hear up to 500 words per minute. The subsequent attempt by our mind to compensate for the remaining 275 words can cause distractions.

As a result, when we are speaking with others, our body language often communicates a lot, particularly when our brain is still trying to fill in the blanks from everything that was said but wasn't said.

Here are some common body language cues and what they mean.

1. Face-to-Face communication.

A steady gaze for a few seconds at a time is regarded as good eye contact. Making a good first impression can be facilitated by maintaining eye contact.

On the other hand, when someone is unhappy and tries to hide it by smiling, they might expose their ruse by looking down. This may also indicate discomfort or shame.

2. Hands that are restless.

Have you ever noticed someone drumming with their fingers on a chair or desk, or even on their legs? These behaviors can indicate impatience, restlessness, and occasionally even anger. When someone does this while you are talking to them, it is time to change your strategy.

3. Leg sluggishness.

Similar to restless hands, but affecting the legs instead of the hands. Legs may be repeatedly crossed and uncrossed, or people may tap their heels or feet.

Remember that some people may experience restless legs due to restless leg syndrome when you notice restless legs everywhere. An urge to move your legs while lying still is associated with this medical condition, which is followed by relief once you move or stand up.

4. Hands on Hips.

If your significant other or your boss at work is standing with their hands on their hips when you approach them, you are in big trouble. Avoid putting your hands on your hips during tense or challenging conversations at work because people interpret this gesture as intimidating.

Keep your hands down and open unless that is what you want to do. This is a more effective strategy for maintaining the peace and the flow of dialogue.

5. One's Head Turning.

People may assume confusion is the meaning when someone tilts their head. This isn't always the situation.

You can show that you are interested in what someone has to say by tilting your head to the side. [2] Be sure to take into account the context of this interaction, including its location and purpose.

6. behind your back, holding your hands.

This is the one that is the most ambiguous among the body language clues on this list. For a variety of reasons, people often hold their hands behind their backs.

You can see Don giving the power sign by holding his hands behind his back in any mafia film. Military personnel are instructed to do it as a sign of respect. Usually, when this happens, you have to rely on other clues to figure out what emotion is being shown.

7. Hands Balled Into Fists.

    This is yet another extremely well-liked indicator. This one essentially has a single meaning, in contrast to the previous one. People act in this way to convey their frustration through body language.

    Due to the fact that balled-up firsts frequently end with something being punched or hit, this is typically a sign of impending violence. When someone's hands are balled into fists while you are speaking with them, things could go very wrong very quickly.

8. Touching.

    Though it can vary greatly, this body language has a universal meaning. This can also be communicated in a variety of ways, such as a boss patting you on the shoulder, a partner resting their head on your shoulder, or a coworker giving you a high-five.

    It makes them feel more at ease around you when someone is touching you without using any force. Even one of the five love languages, affective touch has the power to make the other person feel good.

9. a cross of arms.

    Crossing one's arms actually means something different to many people. It is perceived as a sign of anger. Actually, it's used as a defense mechanism against anxiety and distress.

When someone crosses their arms, it may be because they are tired of talking or because they are trying to hide something. Arms crossed denotes discomfort and a person's attempt to comfort themselves.

10. looking upward.

When you look up, you might be lying and using your imagination, according to some experts. [5] On the other hand, it could also be a sign of joy, happiness, or relief.

What is the first thing an athlete does when they win a game, score a point, or do something great? Usually, they look up. However, there are frequently other signs that appear before that to indicate someone is frustrated. It's true that people can also look upward when they're frustrated. Nevertheless, "chin up!" is used for a reason.

11. Just how near are they?

Many people miss out on a common body language indicator called physical proximity. People won't mind sitting or standing close to you if they feel at ease around you. So going up to someone and brushing shoulders with them is an intriguing way to find out if they actually believe you're okay. If they retreat, you already know the solution!

12. Surprise!

This one should go without saying, but we're talking about common body language signals. Most frequently, when someone widens their eyes or raises their eyebrows, it indicates surprise or shock. [6].

There aren't really any other explanations for someone's eyes to widen. This one is therefore not only very well-liked but also very clear and simple to spot.

13. scanning the area.

There are numerous ways for people to express boredom. One method is to simply wander around when they're bored. When you're conversing with someone and they keep looking around, they are probably looking for something else to do.

This is almost always a bad sign, especially when you're out talking to someone at the bar or, even worse, when you're in a board meeting at work and everyone in the room is engaging in it. Be aware that since smartphones have become so common, people may now pull out their phone and check their email or social networking sites while you're speaking to them. This has a nearly identical meaning.

14. This Stomp.

Although adults are also prone to stomping around, children tend to do this one the most. Most people associate it with being done in a way that expresses anger.

However, there is another reason why people stomp, and that is to intimidate. Stomping can be employed as a method of startling people or even animals. How often do owners stomp close to their dogs to frighten them off?

15. Cleaning Your Throat.

There are many different reasons why people clear their throats. Sometimes you might be ill and have something stuck in your back. However, when someone is nervous or anxious in a perfectly normal social setting, they frequently clear their throats. You will frequently see stand-up comics cough or clear their throat into the microphone if no one is laughing at their jokes while you are watching them. Additionally, people use it to express annoyance.

16. Putting Your Chest Out.

The act of sticking out one's chest can convey strength and confidence. Sticking your chest out is referred to as a power pose when done with your hands on your hips and your chin raised.

Your self-assurance and ability to manage stress can both increase when you jut out your chest in this way. [7] If you adopt this power pose, people will perceive you as strong and capable.

17. Watch Your Steps.

People who move with purpose and vigor appear more assured. A person running is obviously rushing to get somewhere (or away from something).

Walking with a defensive, timid, or disengaged posture is slouching and slumping. According to the experts, success depends on having good posture because it's important in social situations. [8] Even though we may take our posture for granted, there are exercises that can help.

18. Your Eyes are Closed.

Today's sitcoms have made closing your eyes a very common body language cue. The majority of the time, people use it to express their impatience, frustration, and irritability, as if they were mentally reorganizing to tackle a challenge once more.

However, due to its frequent use in comedic situations, some may attempt to use it as a comedy-enhancing device. Typically, the differences are obvious.

19. Rubbing Your Eyes.

If you're speaking with someone and they remove their glasses, pinch the bridge of their nose, and rub their eyes, they are probably not happy with something you just said. Generally speaking, this body language is used to express feelings of exhaustion.

As children constantly rub their eyes when they are tired, this is typically done from a young age.

20. Staring.

Believe it or not, there are two reasons why people stare. Attraction is the main one, as a man or woman may frequently gaze at someone they're attracted to.

However, a lesser known second reason people stare is for dominance. [9] If you're staring down someone and they're staring back, the first to break the stare is considered to be the less dominant one.

Final Thoughts.

The head, eyes, posture, torso, arms, legs, hands, and feet, as well as walking, talking with your hands, and pretty much every motion your body makes have the potential to convey an emotion. The biggest problem is that most people don't know that body language can be so sensitive.

What's even more amazing about body language is its use. In many cases, especially at job interviews, potential employers can analyze your body language to see if you're confident in yourself. At the risk of sounding cliché, everyone everywhere uses body language to show their true feelings. Once you learn what to look for, actions can literally speak louder than words.

Of course, we're talking about listening with your eyes. It's equally important to listen with your ears too, or you can still miss what's really going on.

Humans can spot small signs of sickness at a glance, research suggests.

Coughing, sneezing and clutching the stomach might be obvious signs of sickness, but humans can also spot if someone is healthy simply from a glance at their face, new research suggests.

Scientists have found that signs of a person being acutely unwell – such as pale lips, a downward turn of the mouth and droopy eyelids – are visible just hours after an infection begins.

"We use a number of facial cues from other people and we probably judge the health in other people all the time," said John Axelsson, a co-author of the research and a professor at the stress research institute at Stockholm University.

While previous work has shown that besides overt symptoms – such as sniffing – changes in skin colour can serve as a guide to health, experts say the latest study highlights the ways in which humans might use a host of early signals to avoid contracting infection from others.

Writing in the journal Proceedings of the Royal Society B, Axelsson and colleagues described how they injected 16 healthy adults with a placebo and, at a separate point in time, molecules from E coli which are known to rapidly trigger flu-like symptoms. The participants were unaware which injection they had received, and were photographed about two hours after each injection.

The team then showed the portraits to 62 participants who were asked to judge whether the pictured person was sick or healthy, with each picture shown for a maximum of five seconds.

The results reveal that the participants were able to spot a sick person slightly better than if they were guessing, correctly identifying someone as being unwell 52 percent of the time. However, more impressively, they correctly labelled individuals as being healthy 70 percent of the time.

Axelsson said the judgement of whether someone was sick or healthy might vary depending on the people analyzing the images, noting that people looking for a partner might be better at spotting signs of health, while those afraid of catching an infection might be better at noticing cues for sickness. "I think it depends a bit on the context you are in, on what you are sensitive for," he said. In adulthood, people who are not happy with something will often use that body language to show it.

In order to delve deeper, a brand-new group of 60 participants was shown the pictures without being informed as to which injection had been administered.

On average, people who were photographed after receiving the E coli molecules were rated as looking sicker and more exhausted than people who were photographed after receiving the placebo. Additionally, they were noted to have a paler complexion, more drooping lips, hanging eyelids, redder eyes, and less glossy and patchy skin.

However, further investigation revealed that paler skin and droopier eyelids were most consistently associated with how sick a person was perceived to be.

The research was welcomed, according to Professor Ben Jones of the Face Research Lab at the University of Glasgow. "This study adds to mounting evidence for the presence of facial cues associated with acute sickness and aids in our understanding of how, regrettably, social stigmas about those with illnesses may develop," the author said.

However, he pointed out that the study did not reflect real life, where even the same person's face can exhibit a wide range of variation. Additionally, because other studies have used the same collection of images, caution was advised when drawing conclusions from a small sample of people.

Concerns regarding the small number of individuals who had been photographed were also voiced by Dr. Carmen Lefevre of the University College London center for behavior change. She nonetheless asserted that the research backs the notion that humans have evolved a variety of behavioral mechanisms to aid in disease avoidance. This study is the first to demonstrate that an illness can be identified soon after it manifests, the author continued.

Although the results suggested sick people could be identified quickly after infection, Dr. Rachel McMullan of the Open University added that it would be useful to examine whether the results held for a wide range of ethnic groups and for various diseases.

This study is a good starting point for more research into how we recognize early signs of infection, she added. "Being able to quickly identify and avoid potentially sick, contagious individuals will certainly be an evolutionary advantage," she said.

10 tips for leaders on body language for soft skills.

Even when speaking one-on-one, body language is important in leadership communication. Amy Cuddy's TED Talk on power poses, which has received more than 50 million views, provides an illuminating illustration of the importance of soft skills. In it and her follow-up book on body-mind effects, Cuddy discusses how even small changes in body language can have a significant impact on how people perceive others and themselves.

Sadly, a two-minute Wonder Woman pose is insufficient for leaders to become experts in nonverbal communication. Body language needs constant practice in order to improve, just like other soft skills.

Anne Baum, author of Small Mistakes, Big Consequences: Develop Your Soft Skills to Help You Succeed, claims that despite being one of the most crucial ways we interact with others, body language is likely the skill that people pay the least attention to. It is vitally important to take into account your body language because it conveys nonverbal cues that may contradict what is being said verbally. ".

According to Leila Bulling Towne, executive coach at The Bulling Towne Group, LLC, leaders have an even stronger incentive to develop this skill. As your title increases, you typically become more physically distant from other people and the everyday operations of the business or office, she says. "You could be on a particular floor or in a particular office building. Less people are noticing you. Unbeknownst to you, how you move your hands, body, and eyes—or lack thereof—when your team or those who report into your function do see you—has a greater influence than you might think. Since they don't often watch you, when they do, they carefully scrutinize your words and deeds. " .

We solicited advice and recommendations from leaders, executive coaches, and body language experts. Continue reading to find out how to use your body language to your advantage. We'll wrap up by discussing how to assess your own body language.

1. Choose the message you want to deliver.

Edward Schiappa, professor of comparative media studies at MIT and coordinator of MIT Professional Education's upcoming Persuasive Communications Boot camp: "Almost everything we do — how we move, talk, gesture, look at people, shake hands, sit down, set up our office. dress, wear our hair, etc. — is a form of communication. – expresses a characteristic of who we are. Therefore, the first crucial step for leaders to think about is: Who is the "I" that I present to my peers and teams? Am I communicating the qualities that I want to communicate?

"Consider how we convey credibility: Making eye contact, demonstrating respect and confidence in teammates or peers, and showing support in a conversation nonverbally. Leaning backward or forward in a chair has a literal impact; one suggests distance while the other conveys interest and involvement. Therefore, how you carry yourself physically has a huge impact. In other words, the error to avoid is adopting body language that is inconsistent with the behavior that characterizes the leader you want to be. ".

2. Keep being yourself.

According to Elizabeth Gilbert, a researcher at PsychologyCompass.com, "There is no one approach that works for everyone. Instead, adapt your nonverbal communication to both yourself and your audience. When practicing your body language, keep in mind who you are speaking with and what you want to say. Communication is a social experience. Use expansive body language (think "man spreading") and large gestures, for instance, to convey authority. Consider making subtler gestures and taking up less physical space if you want to be friendly and make people feel at ease.

In addition, you should feel at ease when communicating nonverbally. This is not to say that you can't get better at non-verbal communication; you can and should work on new behaviors like physically leaning in, striking a pose of power, using complementary hand gestures, etc. However, if you consistently act like an outgoing, loud extrovert when in reality you're a more reserved introvert (or vice versa), this can be detrimental to your wellbeing. Additionally, it might seem insincere. So think about how to align your nonverbal behavior with your true self. ".

3. Between open and closed body language, strike a balance.

"Managers can err on either extreme of the spectrum. With their body language, they can be overly forthcoming and eager, which frequently causes teams and employees to feel uneasy. For instance, adopting a power pose can help presenters feel more assured, but it can also come across as haughty in certain situations (like when you're the most important person in the room).

The team members may also think their manager doesn't care if they are too distant or closed off, which will happen occasionally. The team would be uncertain about any decision made by a leader who keeps their head down because they are frequently perceived as meek or doubtful. Be calm and aware of the messages your body language is conveying in this situation. ".

4. Show that you are paying attention.

Speak Clear Communications executive speech coach Jeffrey Davis: "It's crucial for executives to show their staff members that they are present and paying attention. Simple actions can make a difference, such as sitting up straight, maintaining eye contact, gesturing with open hands, and keeping your fingertips lightly in contact while resting your hands. You should use your nonverbal communication to convey the values of listening, relating, and emotional connection. Any gesture or movement that goes against these principles, such as crossing one's arms or slouching one's shoulders, should be avoided. ".

5. Making eye contact fosters trust.

A leader must make eye contact constantly. Building trust between a leader and their team members involves looking them in the eyes, listening to them rather than just responding, and speaking slowly and clearly. A leader comes across as disinterested or uncaring when they are not paying attention to the team. It makes no difference what is said because this undermines trust. ".

6. Keep both hands free.

"Remain open with your hands. Unexpectedly, clenching your hands or making fists increases your body tension as well as the tension you project to others. Excellent leaders are receptive to others' opinions and ideas. Your body and mind need to be open for you to remain open. To physically remind yourself to maintain an open mind during meetings, presentations, and negotiations, open your hands.

Also, refrain from touching your face with your hands. You'd be surprised how frequently people forget to keep their hands off their faces during meetings, even though this advice shouldn't need to be repeated to anyone past elementary school. Disgust has a tremendous amount of power; in fact, it has the ability to dominate almost any other emotion experienced during a meeting. So keep your head up and your hands down.

8 effective sentences from emotionally intelligent leaders.

Add these short, effective phrases to your leadership vocabulary to practice emotional intelligence.

It's easy to identify leaders who have emotional intelligence because it's a soft skill that they absolutely must have. Leaders with high EQ attract followers. Their interactions with coworkers give it away. Even the language they use on a daily basis exhibits high emotional intelligence.

According to Jonathan Feldman, CIO of the city of Asheville, NC, "emotionally intelligent people want to know that their boss is emotionally intelligent, as well.". "That typically translates into wanting to see some self-awareness. The use of expressions like "I was wrong," "Oh, you're right," and "I fell short on that one by not doing XYZ" can help employees understand this. " .

The eight most effective words for emotionally intelligent leadership.

Consider carefully the language you use with coworkers as you strive to become more self-aware of your own emotions. Here are eight more words you can start adding to your leadership vocabulary right away to establish more meaningful connections with and rapport with your team. Additionally, it goes beyond mere platitudes. Daniel Goleman argued that emotional intelligence outperformed cognitive intelligence as the best predictor of business success in his 1995 best seller Emotional Intelligence.

Fortunately, emotional intelligence is one of those leadership abilities that gets better with continued use. These short but effective sentences are a great place to start.

Please elaborate. ".

Leaders who are emotionally intelligent frequently have communication expertise, which is a crucial soft skill. They are also aware that it might be difficult for others, and they would never draw conclusions from a coworker's comments. According to Dr. Neeta Bhushan, emotional health educator and author of "Emotional GRIT," asking "Tell me more about that" or "What did you mean when you said/did that?" is a judgment-free way to gain clarity. According to her, when leaders use these words, they are acting from an attitude of curiosity and compassion rather than condemnation.

According to Drew Bird, founder of The EQ Development Group, "the phrase 'can you say more about that' demonstrates a desire to better understand what the other person is saying or trying to get at, but is non-evaluative.".

What is your preferred method of communication?

 | *Understanding All Body Sign and Language*

Additionally, leaders with high EQ don't presume to know how others prefer to be communicated with. For instance, some people might value face-to-face interactions while others might favor a straightforward text message. In order to customize their communication style for each member of their team, emotionally intelligent leaders are interested in learning about these preferences.

"Leaders who possess emotional intelligence are adept at empathetic communication. And they understand that in order to do so, they must get to know the other person and inquire as to how they prefer to receive information," writes Colin D. Ellis, author of "The Conscious Project Leader. Humans have different preferences for how we should be communicated with, so high-EQ leaders will always inquire. ".

"Thanks for your help. "

Leaders who possess emotional intelligence excel when providing feedback. "Looks good," says Sanjay Malhotra, CTO of Clearbridge Mobile. " .

He acknowledges, "I know it sounds easy. "Day in and day out, my team works to produce work and products they can be proud of. Due to the fact that there are frequently competing projects and priorities, I try to let everyone know that they are appreciated, even if only briefly. Despite how insignificant it may seem, I know how much it means to my team to hear that their efforts have paid off. " .

However, it's not just for the team. Effective leaders who use this expression develop deeper bonds of trust with their team members, which benefits everyone. According to Bhushan, "Expressing gratitude and acceptance is a surefire way to have positive engagement and employee satisfaction.".

While it's nice to hear "good job," Bird argues that adding some context makes it even more meaningful. It's more meaningful than just saying "thanks," he says, "if you can help people understand why you are grateful.". I really appreciate you doing that because [insert the impact of their actions]," Bird suggests. ".

I want to know what you think.

For high-EQ leaders, Ellis asserts, feedback is a two-way street. According to him, inclusive leaders are by nature always looking for ways to include the opinions and ideas of others in a conversation. They seek out opportunities to elevate others because they are aware that they are not the smartest person in the room. "

"I view things differently. ".

Leaders with high EQ don't avoid challenging discussions. Instead, they take the opportunity presented by disagreements to open communication and seek out common ground.

I have a different perspective is a more emotionally intelligent way to say "I don't agree," according to Bird. "Having a different perspective simply means that you have a different understanding of this chance or challenge. ".

When those divergent points of view result in disagreement, Bird suggests using the phrase: "It makes me [insert emotion/feeling] when you dot. According to Bird, "This language shows that the leader has thought about what is happening and allows the other person to hear the impact of their actions.".

"Are you OK."

The majority of people experience ebbs and flows in their creative abilities. Sometimes we're on full-throttle, and other times we need a few extra cups of coffee to get through the workday. This is something that emotionally intelligent managers are aware of and they do. Additionally, they make sure to check in on the wellbeing of the staff.

There are times when people are unable to be the most effective versions of themselves. The response of emotionally intelligent leaders in these situations is not to chastise them for missing a deadline or allowing the quality of their work to slip. It is to compassionately inquire about their well-being, according to Ellis. "This is just one way they demonstrate that they are concerned primarily with other people's well-being. ".

You are heard. ".

Emotional intelligence is characterized by empathy, as noted by Ellis. As well, Bhushan. The best way to demonstrate emotional intelligence, show that you are listening to the other person, and show that you are not acting with ulterior motives is to demonstrate empathy, according to the expert.

She advises using expressions like "I hear you" and "I understand" to help you build your vocabulary of empathic words.

"I'm sorry."

Leaders who have a strong emotional intelligence don't hesitate to accept their mistakes. According to Bird, apologizing in an open and sincere way reveals a high level of emotional intelligence because it exhibits a modesty and humility that followers greatly value.

According to Ellis, humility is essential: "Humility is a key behavioral trait of emotionally intelligent leaders. They are self-aware enough to realize when they've said or done something that has angered or devalued another person, and they are determined to make amends as soon as possible, he says.

Pandemic leadership that is emotionally intelligent.

It's crucial to focus on developing personal relationships as a leader, as Janele Lynn, owner of the Lynn Leadership Group, recently noted, particularly at this time when team members are dealing with the COVID-19 pandemic's effects and getting ready for what comes next.

"The novelty of working remotely has seriously faded. According to Lynn, "The new normal has simply become the new normal, and we're not necessarily thinking about how to support our people as they adjust, but rather, we're just focused on doing our jobs. Because of this, we might neglect some of the more time-consuming aspects of leadership. ".

Chapter 11:

Summary

Various body language types.

We have significant categories of body language.

Body language is the tacit method of communication we used to convey our true feelings and lend more credibility to what we say.

More than just words are involved in communication. Nonverbal cues like posture, gestures, and voice inflection all matter.

Simple examples of body language include a relaxed facial expression that turns into an honest smile, with the mouth turned up and the eyes wrinkled. A head tilt to convey thought, a straight posture to convey interest, or hand and arm motions to convey directions are other examples. Avoiding adopting a defensive stance with your arms crossed or erratic foot tapping would be another illustration.

Being able to "read" such signs allows you to fully understand what someone is saying. Additionally, you will be more aware of the reactions of others to your actions and words.

You'll be able to alter your body language as well to project an upbeat, intriguing, and approachable impression.

By paying attention to how you stand, sit, and move, you can discover more about who you are. All people express their body language through one of four movements: precise and bold, dynamic and determined, soft and fluid, or light and bouncy.

Every movement has a distinct meaning and is associated with one of the four different types of energy. Energy Profiling is a method of identifying an individual based on movement that leads with a dominant Energy Type like everything in our natural environment. The two most reliable methods of assessment for identifying your Energy Type are your facial features and your body language.

Energy of Type 1 is upward, light, and animated.

Your gait is buoyant and springy as you move. When you're standing or sitting, you move around a lot and switch positions frequently.

You might come across as restless to others because you find it difficult to sit still or focus on one thing for an extended period. You frequently sit on the floor or comfortably cross your legs.

Fluid, soft energy is of type 2.

With elegance and ease, you stroll. You take more deliberate steps and keep your feet firmly on the ground. Your movements are incredibly fluid and smooth; there is no bounce. When sitting and standing in an S-curve or with a relaxed bend, you hold your head to the side.

Energy of type 3 is reactive, substantial, and active.

You walk quickly and deliberately, putting your feet down firmly. I can hear you coming from a distance. Even as you sit, others can hear you because of your deliberate movements. I created angles when you stand and sit. Legs crossed, one leg lifted in front of you, cocked head, hands on waist, or torso bowed at the waist.

Bold, consistent, still energy is Type 4.

Your gait is very upright, motionless, and stately, and your body and limbs barely move. Additionally, you sit very straight, with your feet flat on the ground, your back straight, and your hands folded or by your sides. Your posture could be considered formal if you were standing or sitting.

Most runway models possess dominant Type 4 Energy; they move with natural erectness, poise, and structure, as well as straight shoulders and ideal posture.

How to interpret nonverbal cues and develop stronger emotional awareness.

Even though we can express ourselves with words and tone of voice, we all speak a distinct language.

And that's body language.

Using nonverbal cues, we can communicate with others more effectively than we can with words. Gestures, facial expressions, and the degree of eye contact all convey meaning.

You can better understand your peers if you can read and interpret body language. To present yourself as you would like to be seen, it is also crucial to be aware of your own body language.

It's not always easy to understand the psychology of body language. However, we're going to help reveal the mysteries of body language signals.

Here's a guide to understanding body language and the meaning of various nonverbal cues.

What does body language mean?

You've successfully read someone's body language if you could tell how they were feeling just by looking at their face or observing their gestures.

The definition of body language referred nonverbal cues that us consciously and unconsciously used to communicate to. Nonverbal communication in general is included.

They composed our verbal communication of the words we use to speak.

A person's body language, which consists of non-verbal cues, frequently conveys more information than their words. These cues could be:

•Facial expressions.

Hand signals.

•Mannerisms.

• Physical activity.

•Voice tonality.

As we explore how to read body language in greater detail below, we'll take a closer s at cues.

We frequently employ nonverbal cues instinctively or unconsciously, which is one of the most significant facts about body language signals.

Because of this, our body language frequently conveys to others more about our thoughts and feelings than our words do.

You can compel the person you're speaking to trust you and feel at ease in your company by using certain body language cues. Alternately, you could offend or confuse them.

Even your spoken words can be undermined or contradicted by the nonverbal communication styles you employ.

Why is it important to interpret body language?

What are the advantages of learning body language interpretation and why is it important?

Looking at the 7-38-55 rule helps us understand the solutions to these queries. This rule is based on research by Albert Mehrabian, a psychology professor. The rule was created in the late 1960s and early 1970s by a professor at the University of California.

The spoken word conveys 7% of meaning, in Mehrabian's estimation. Your body language and voice intonation convey 55% and 38% of the meaning, respectively.

Given how frequently we express ourselves through nonverbal cues, becoming adept at reading body language is a requirement if you're serious about improving your communication skills. Knowing how to interpret body language will help you better understand what other people are trying to say.

You can consciously work on communicating more nonverbally.

Let's examine some advantages of body language comprehension.

1. Increase your emotional intelligence.

You can more accurately decipher other people's emotions and moods by learning to read their body language. This makes it possible for you to discern their true feelings or thoughts.

Then you can react to them properly.

2. Better relationships with your peers.

Sharing one's genuine emotions or thoughts is not always comfortable. There may be issues in the family they are dealing with. Additionally, they might believe that no one would pay attention to them.

You can gain a better understanding of someone's opinions by reading their body language. Or you can be friendly and supportive when they need support, but don't feel that they can ask for it.

3. Create trust more easily.

When you can read body language, you can use it to establish trust.

You can consciously give off nonverbal cues that you're being sincere and open. The signals that suggest you're preoccupied, dishonest, or concealing something can also be avoided.

4. Get your point across in the right way.

Understanding body language also helps you communicate your ideas more effectively.

5. Make a good impression and influence people.

Consciously using different types of nonverbal communication can help you appear confident, even if you don't feel it. You can also emphasize your message and inspire trust, as mentioned. Altogether, this helps you make a good first impression and builds your influence on others.

How to read body language according to every body part.

Learning how to read body language signals isn't limited to one or two parts of the body.

Familiarize yourself with these parts of the body that offer important insights into a person and their message.

1. Eyes.

I know the eyes as the windows of the soul. They play an important role in face-to-face communication. Take note of body language signs such as.

• Eye contact: a direct gaze indicates interest unless it's prolonged, in which case it can be threatening. Looking away frequently or avoiding eye contact can indicate that the person is uncomfortable, trying to hide something, or distracted.

• Pupil dilation: highly dilated pupils can indicate excitement, attraction, or desire. Constricted, smaller pupils could indicate anger or a negative mood.

• Blinking: frequent blinking can indicate that the person feels uncomfortable or upset.

2. Facial expressions.

Often unconscious, our facial expressions can reveal what we really think about something.

There is no global standard for facial expressions linked to specific emotions. The meaning behind facial expressions depends on context. However, expressions can indicate a range of emotions.

Among them are:.

• Happiness.

• Anger.

• Sadness.

• Confusion.

• Contempt.

• Fear.

• Excitement.

3. Arms.

A person's arms can also be used for non-verbal communication. Body language examples of this include:.

• Keeping the arms close to the body to draw less attention.

• Expanding the arms to appear more commanding, larger, or threatening.

• Crossing the arms to indicate feelings of self-protection, defensiveness, or being closed-off.

4. ft\. and legs.

Our feet and legs aren't the first body parts that come to mind when we think about types of nonverbal communication.

However, they also play a role in body language psychology:.

• Both feet pointed toward you or in a V-shape toward you can indicate interest.

• Both feet pointed away from you, especially in an angled V-shape, can indicate disinterest.

• Crossed legs may indicate the person feels disinterested or closed-off.

5. Hands and fingers.

From excitable hand-flapping to obscene gestures, we can use our hands to express a lot of emotions. Being aware of the hands and fingers is an important part of learning how to read body language.

Examples of using the hands and fingers for nonverbal communication include:.

• Giving a thumbs-up as a sign of approval.

• Using the index and middle fingers to form a forward-facing V-sign to indicate victory.

• Raising a clenched fist to indicate anger or solidarity.

• Clasping hands behind your back to indicate anxiety or boredom.

• Rapidly tapping fingers to express irritation or frustration.

• Standing with hands on the hips to indicate control or aggression.

6. Torso.

The torso also offers a few important body language examples:.

• An erect posture and open torso (rather than being shielded by crossed arms) can show confidence, assertiveness, and attention.

• A slouched posture can indicate boredom, disinterest, and being closed-off.

7. Mouth.

The mouth makes some of the most important body language signs. Examples include:.

• Smiling to show happiness, approval, sarcasm, or cynicism.

• Biting the lower lip to indicate insecurity or worry.

• Covering the mouth to hide a reaction such as a genuine smile or smirk.

• Pursing the lips to indicate disapproval, distrust, or annoyance.

 Understanding All Body Sign and Language

5 ways to read positive body language.

Knowing how to read positive body language can help you in business and social contexts. Here are a few things to look out for:.

1. Having good posture.

If someone is sitting up straight, it's a sign they're paying attention to what you're saying. An open posture also indicates friendliness.

2. Maintaining eye contact .

There's a difference between maintaining eye contact and staring or glaring.

If someone makes a healthy amount of direct eye contact with you, it means they're engaged in the conversation and paying attention. It's normal for them to blink and look away occasionally.

If someone stares or glares at you, it's usually not a positive sign.

3. Leaning in to listen.

Various body language signs indicate that someone is listening to what you're saying. If their head and torso are turned in your direction and they're leaning toward you, it means they're listening.

Other positive signs include nodding their head, sitting with arms and legs uncrossed, and aiming an ear in your direction.

4. Keeping the body still.

If a person's body is still, it can mean they're relaxed. It can also indicate that they're focused and paying attention to what you're saying.

If the person's emotion or attitude isn't clear from how still their body is, look at the other types of nonverbal behavior on display.

5. A firm handshake.

If someone gives you a firm handshake, it's a sign that they respect you.

If they were the one to reach out to shake hands, they probably have healthy self-confidence. A firm handshake should not be painful, as that can be intimidating.

5 ways to read negative body language.

Your knowledge of body language psychology should also include negative signs.

When you can recognize the following signs in your audience, you can change tactics or express your message in another way.

If you become aware that you're using negative nonverbal cues, you can consciously change them to positive cues. This is a way of supporting or encouraging the speaker by letting them know you're interested — or by disguising the fact that you're not interested.

In situations where discretion is best, you can use negative types of nonverbal communication to express distrust, disinterest, or disapproval.

Negative body language examples include:

1. Bad posture or slouching.

If the person you're communicating with is slouched or tense, it's a sign that they're bored. They might also feel disinterested, threatened, or worried.

You can use verbal and nonverbal cues to reassure them or to regain their interest.

2. Avoiding eye contact.

If someone avoids making eye contact with you, it could be a negative sign for one or more reasons.

Having a lot of eye movement and not making eye contact may indicate that they're disinterested or distracted. They might be trying to hide something, or they feel uncomfortable or guilty.

3. Crossed arms.

Interpreting crossed arms is one of the basics of learning how to read body language, as it's one of the classic negative signs.

Crossed arms are likely to show that the person feels defensive or closed-off to you and your message. It can also indicate aggression or anger.

4. Fidgeting and unable to keep still.

If someone is fidgeting or unable to keep still, it's a sign that they are distracted, bored, or uninterested in what you are saying. Stress can also cause fidgeting.

Common types of fidgeting include foot-tapping, crossing and uncrossing of legs, or consistently playing with an object such as a pen.

5. Negative facial expressions.

A range of facial expressions can indicate negative attitudes or emotions. Recognizing them can help you understand your audience's actual responses to your message.

Frowning may indicate disagreement, anger, or confusion.

Pursed lips usually indicate annoyance, displeasure, and distaste.

Flared nostrils may show aggression or disapproval. Or they can indicate that the person is making a judgment about something.

Upskill yourself by learning how to read body language.

Learning how to read body language, as well as how to use it consciously, is an important soft skill that has many benefits in the workplace and outside of it. Upskilling yourself with powerful communication skills will help you move your career forward.

Reading body language can help you better respond to your audience, whether they're family members, friends, or coworkers. You can tailor your communication to them when you can identify what engages and interests them.

You can use different types of nonverbal communication to:

• Repeat and strengthen your verbal message.

• Complement your verbal message.

• Substitute for a verbal message.

• Accent elements of your message.

Improve your body language understanding with coaching from BetterUp. Building effective communication skills takes time, but the effects are worth the effort both professionally and personally.

Request a custom demo to get started. You can consciously incorporate gestures and other nonverbal cues that emphasize your point rather than contradict it.

Wrapping Up

We all use body language, but very few people are aware of its importance. Only a small percentage of people are aware that reading body language can give us access to a person's innermost thoughts and that we can also use it to shape our own perceptions of others.

Our goal in writing this e-Book was to shed light on some of the most crucial facets of body language interpretation. We require this and ought to make use of it in order to make the best possible impression, develop personally, give others what we want to give them, and learn about what's on people's minds.

Effective body language reading can help us in many different aspects of our lives, including helping us develop stronger personalities. We improve our conversational skills. From people, we can learn the information we seek. Speaking skills can be improved. Improved team management is something we can achieve. We can develop as teachers. The ability to read body language can be extremely helpful to us almost everywhere in our lives. We can be more content with our lives and have better businesses and relationships.

Use the methods in this e-Book to reinvent your life.